The
Apprentice
Property
Master

PAUL
TORRISI

Finalist in series 1 of BBC TV's hugely popular 'The Apprentice', Paul Torrisi tells the story of how he built the property business that made him too successful for Sir Alan Sugar!

The Apprentice Property Master

 Spring Hill

Published by Spring Hill

Spring Hill in an imprint of
How To Books Ltd
Spring Hill House
Spring Hill Road
Begbroke, Oxford OX5 1RX, United Kingdom
Tel: (01865) 375794. Fax: (01865) 379162
info@howtobooks.co.uk
www.howtobooks.co.uk

The right of Paul Torrisi to be identified as the author of this work
has been asserted by him in accordance with the Copyright,
Designs and Patents Act 1988.

© **Paul Torrisi 2008**

British Library Cataloguing in Publication Data
A catalogue record for this book is available from the British
Library

ISBN 978 1 905862 18 4

Cover design by Baseline Arts Ltd, Oxford
Produced for How to Books by Deer Park Productions, Tavistock
Typeset by Pantek Arts Ltd, Maidstone, Kent
Printed and bound by Cromwell Press, Trowbridge, Wiltshire

NOTE: The material contained in this book is set out in good
faith for general guidance and no liability can be accepted
for loss or expense incurred as a result of relying in particular
circumstances on statements made in this book. Laws and
regulations are complex and liable to change, and readers should
check the current position with the relevant authorities before
making personal arrangements.

Contents

Introduction

'Paul you're too successful for me. You've got your own company and you're doing very well. Why would you want to come and work for me?'

Sir Alan Sugar *The Apprentice* BBC2

When you were a kid (assuming you're not one now), what where you doing in your summer holidays? I bet I know. If your dad worked for a company, then you would have done what most kids do in the holidays; dossed around and had a good time. But if your dad had his own firm, then I bet he took you to work with him, just like my dad did with me.

At first I thought it was going to be a bit of a lark, messing about in a textile factory: climbing up things, getting money from people just for having a cheeky face. But the reality, shall we say, was a little different. The second I walked in I was put to work. My dad saw to it that I did jobs that were integral to production: not clearing out cupboards, or serving in the canteen. I, therefore, had a sense of purpose, knowing that whatever job I did was important. My dad, I'm sure you have just realised, was crafty. I couldn't pull a sickie, or play on Atari, otherwise I'd get 'Who is going to do your job today? The order will be late and all the staff will suffer.' It seemed this eight-year-old boy was indispensable, a key person, fundamental to the company. My dad's factory just couldn't manage without me (apart from when I went back to school then somehow miraculously the factory survived!). Anyway, I worked in every single school holiday from when I was eight until I was 16.

Having spent so much time in that factory, I knew the staff, the layout, what was manufactured and basically how it was made. The firm seemed to be doing OK – at home we had food on the table and went on foreign holidays. As I was the only son and my sister showed no interest in the factory, I guess it was the unspoken rule that one day I would join and then perhaps take over and pretty much enjoy the same life that my parents had had. My dad, however, always kidded himself that I was to become a doctor or a lawyer. I say 'kidded', because I was not doctor or lawyer material. I knew that your foot bone was connected to your ankle bone, and that if you were caught stealing you were nicked, but I couldn't make a career out of knowing that, could I?

Although I did do my best at school, and got OK grades at 'O' level, I just knew that when I went into the real world I would not be able to rely on school or university qualifications to earn my living. So I didn't bother trying for 'A' levels, and hence a place at a uni was out of the equation. But I also thought that although the factory beckoned it was a little too soon for that, and that the sensible thing to do was go to London and enjoy myself… so I did.

I didn't know this at the time, but enjoying yourself costs money. I knew that no qualifications to speak of would greatly reduce the type of jobs that I could go for. I still didn't think that there was going to be any real problem though for a bright, handsome, witty, intelligent young man… oh, give me the 'handsome' at least. I was in London: how could I not find a job in London? Fortunately, I knew someone who knew someone who was looking for a handsome (as agreed) 17 year old who didn't mind working his tail off. That someone was the sales manager at the Ford Motor Company and I went for a job as a van and truck salesman in Wandsworth.

The job suited me down to the ground. I had always considered myself a bit of a wheeler-dealer. From the age of 11 I went to boarding school and my mother used to make me all sorts of cakes and goodies to see me through until the next leave-out weekend, which would be three weeks away. I very quickly discovered that on certain evenings, other schoolboys would pay the earth for these little goodies. At the time there was a curfew in place which meant that no one could leave school grounds after 6.30pm, and as we all know people always get the munchies after that. So, at the age of 11, I knew all about supply and demand. I had a lucrative sideline selling these wares to my friends, and the money I was earning was helping to fund my ever growing electric guitar collection.

Six years later

I got the job.

'Sales' is all about commission. The strategy, therefore, is to pay your sales team a low wage, but not so low that it is insulting. Nor can it be so low that if you have a bad month, as we all do, life itself would be almost intolerable. Find the happy medium and then load up the commission, the incentive to sell. But money aside, the day I started my first real job, outside of the family, I realised that I loved it. For me it wasn't work. When I woke up on any given Monday, I looked forward to going in. Work started at 9am, and I would be there at 7.30am. This was something new. But I impressed myself by getting the job in the first place on nothing more than enthusiasm. When I went for the job, I didn't know the salary or the commission scale – I thought it would all be much of a muchness. Thus when I got the job, I was alarmed to hear that the basic wage was £75 per week. I had had the job for about one minute before I put in for my first pay rise:

'I have got to have at least £100 per week; it will cost me a tenner a week on the bus to get to work.'

I got my £100 per week. I won't bore you with the details of the commission's sliding scale but it went from 10 per cent to 16.5 per cent depending on the profit I made on each deal. Fair enough.

I started the following Monday. I had an office that I shared with two other salesmen, both of whom were in their thirties, and we had a secretary called Elaine that we all shared (no sniggering). All the sales team worked from a batch of cards that had all the pertinent information about particular companies and, ergo, potential customers. Hundreds of them. As we called the companies it would be up to us to write remarks on the cards about how the call went and if they were in the market for new vehicles or not.

Picking up the phone and cold calling these companies was not an issue for me, but I saw that it was for the other two. They would do anything to not cold call. Writing out quotes for other companies, shuffling pieces of paper, but not actually picking up the phone. As it turned out, these two were hopeless. I saw that in an instant. Even Elaine, a wonderful chatty lass in her thirties from Manchester, told me that there were concerns higher up about these two. They made a big deal about something that should have been easy. They would gear themselves up for a phone call. So instead of making 50 calls a day, they would make three. I could further drum home the point by using a football analogy and suggest that the more shots your team have on goal, the more likely it is that they will score. I happen to adopt that theory. However, it was·not the place of a smug 17 year old to offer advice to these two seasoned campaigners, so I kept my thoughts to myself. But the difference was that coming to work for these two was a chore, for me it was a joy.

Why did I love it?

I found it easy, simple as that. It has to be said that I had the sort of personality that leant itself to adapt and manipulate to suit any given situation. Of course I did not know this at the time, nor did I know that this was indeed the main reason for my selling ability.

Any customer was fair game, whether it was DHL Couriers or a sole trader, we as salespeople were encouraged to go after everyone and had to be capable and ready to deal with them all, speaking to them in their own language. I have a theory that there are basically two types of sales that a person will encounter:

1 easy

2 hard.

Easy: a customer approaches *you*. Hard: *you* cold call them.

This little story says it all. Some years ago my car broke down and as it was already on its last legs, fixing it (again) was not really financially viable. I had to bite the bullet and buy another one. I needed it sharpish too, as I worked 30 miles from where I lived. As luck would have it, it was Christmas Eve, pelting with snow and all the second-hand car dealerships were closed. Finally I found one that was not only open but looked to have the ilk of car that I wanted within my budget. When the salesman (more likely owner: who else would work Christmas Eve?) approached me, he said, 'Well at least I know you're serious.' He had me right where he wanted me, and the £250 discount that he gave me on the four-year-old Fiat Uno was more out of Christmas charity than hard negotiating by me. What I am saying here is that how you are approached will dictate how you will proceed. That salesman could have sold me anything at any price, because he knew I was desperate (he wouldn't have got any repeat business, but I think he was just interested in some extra cash for Christmas).

Finding the business

Now, when you as the salesperson have to go and find the business, *that* is a different story. That is what really separates the men from the boys. No matter how you go about it, the one thing you absolutely have to have in massive amounts is 'bottle', and just a little bit of knowledge. Picking up the phone to a potential punter is nerve wracking because you have no idea who will be at the other end or what mood they will be in. Remember, a potential customer in the wrong frame of mind approached by a salesperson without the experience to realise it means any hope of a deal is dead in the water. If you pick up the phone, then dial, and the person at the other end picks up and says 'What?!', put the phone down. Don't even try to say a word, otherwise they will associate you with the mood that they are already in. So when you call back, even if they are feeling better, you are psychologically on the back foot.

I am a big advocate of experience in the field and using common sense in the workplace. Common sense is something we all have, in varying amounts, and experience does not have to have been gleaned from decades of apprenticeship. I started work on a Monday; by Tuesday I had sold my first truck and learned everything that there was to learn in 24 hours.

You've probably by this stage worked out the sort of guy I was and still am. Let me elaborate a little more: that first truck that I sold was to a company called Hirus, in Watford. They had a large fleet of Transits and on their card it simply stated that they bought Ford Transit Populars at 16.5 per cent discount. At which point I knew that discussing anything else with these people would be fruitless. I called them and asked to speak to John. The secretary asked who was calling and I replied, 'Paul from Hunts', as if John and I spoke every day at the golf club. Within two seconds the owner of this multi-million pound company was on the line to a 17-year-old lad, who yesterday didn't know what a Transit van was. This is how the call went:

'Mr Gregory, it's Paul from Hunts. We have just taken delivery of two Transit chassis cabs, both Populars and both petrol. I know they are the sort you like; I can of course do them at 16.5 per cent. With the Ford price rise in two months I thought I would offer them to you now. You obviously want them before the price rise?'

'Obviously. Get them prepped, and then send them down. Who are you again?'

'Paul. Hunt Trucks. Wandsworth.'

'OK. Thanks Paul.'

Deal done. Everything that came out of my mouth was instinctive. I didn't plan the call – no point really as I had no idea who Mr Gregory was or the mood I would find him in. So I stuck to a couple of basic principles:

- I should do most of the talking
- I should offer him something that is easy to say yes to.

Starting over

For the next three years I was very happy selling trucks. I was put in charge of the entire used division when I was just 19 years old (eight years after I first started selling my mum's mince pies to my friends at boarding school), and continued to enjoy the whole experience. What I got up to in the three years I was there is a book itself. Then, it was over.

The big cheese, and I really mean the big cheese too, called all the staff into his office to use the most awful words an employee can ever hear from an employer: 'Get out of my parking spot for good.' I'm only joking… 'cutbacks'. We would, none of us, lose our jobs (we couldn't as we were sales and so kept the company, any company, going). Basic salaries, however, would be halved, or in my case cut by 66 per cent (when I, however, realised that I was selling more trucks than people three times my age, it didn't take long for me to realise my worth and demand a pay rise). This was 1990, the beginning of the great recession. I had rent to pay, even if it was a lowly one-bedroom flat with no central heating, so I gave it some thought and decided that three years in London was enough, and I called my parents to say that I was coming home.

I put in my notice and left London on the last Friday of May 1990. The following Monday I was in at my father's factory, where I knew I would always end up. Within three months of arriving, however, my father gave me some advice that made me think that all those working holidays in the factory had been in vain.

1
Getting Started in Property Investment

The state of manufacturing in this country has been in steady decline really since the Seventies. The trade unions gave employees the right to have power over their bosses. If something was not going quite to their liking, strike! Factories are really the only working environments where people congregate *en masse* to do their job. Consequently strike action means that large groups of people stop working. It was, therefore, inevitable that large factories were very inefficient as they had to constantly make up for lost time.

Smaller factories without powerful unions were not affected in the same way; they could be productive and competitive, as they were only really competing against other British companies. Our factory fell into this camp. The Seventies and Eighties were a time of boom for most small- to medium-sized companies (SMEs), but much depended on the people in charge and how they ran things. The Nineties were the time when things started to change. Large clothing retailers started to exploit the possibility of manufacturing goods offshore. Lead times had to be increased as the product came from farther away, but the cost saving mitigated the additional transportation costs.

For a certain period in the mid-Nineties, as a direct consequence of foreign imports, 1,000 companies per week were going to the wall. For a great many of these companies and their staff, this was all a sudden blow, but my father, it has to be said, saw the writing on the wall ten years earlier. Although he made noises to me even in the Eighties, it wasn't until 1990 (when I joined the family firm as a man rather than a schoolboy needing pocket money to buy a Gibson Firebird) that he suggested I look for another way of making a living, as this type of industry would not be able to sustain a newcomer for too much longer.

I have to say, hearing that was a bit like spending your young life becoming skilled in petrochemicals only to be told on the day you qualify that the world's oil will run out tomorrow. To start with I didn't do anything. I just started work, becoming certified as a work and method study engineer and trying to get on with the task in hand. But of course in the back of my mind I knew full well that this was not forever. I also had to bear in mind that any financial investment into the factory would have to be minimal: what would be the point in refitting a ship you *know* will sink? But whatever I decided to do, it had to be something that I was capable of doing. I didn't want to bite off more than I could chew.

Looking for an alternative career

I began to search for something else to go into. Sales was the obvious choice as I knew I was good at it, but with the whole world, as it appeared, in recession, companies were not really hiring. Consequently, it occurred to me that I would have to use my own endeavours to get ahead and not be reliant on picking up a salary offered by a northern firm. I began to look for openings: something I could do without having to retrain. I was at the disadvantage of not having gone to university, but when it came to starting your own business this didn't matter. I kept reminding myself of all those stories about Henry Ford and Nelson Rockefeller who had both been expelled from school and left with no qualifications. I wasn't looking to become the Henry Ford of Scunthorpe, maybe just the Nelson Rockefeller.

One thing I did notice was the price difference in property from London to the North.

Scunthorpe, in North Lincolnshire, had one-bedroom flats for sale for £8,500. I made some enquiries and found that they would let for between £50 and £60 per week.

'Wow,' I thought, 'that's your money back in three and a half years.' I also thought that it would be something I could do while I still had a day job.

How hard could it be? Letting out properties then going round each place every Friday night after work to collect your rent. The only real problem was that I didn't have any money to get started. I had a nice collection of electric guitars but no cash. So I did what any sensible son would have done, I went to my dad for help.

Now my dad is no fool, and the fact that I am his son cuts no ice with him either. If I had gone to him asking for financial help for an idiotic idea he would have told me to take a running jump. As it happens, I think he took the idea seriously as any money that I borrowed from him would be borrowed for the acquisition of real bricks and mortar, so if it all went wrong, there would at least be something tangible that could be used against any debt I incurred. So a deal was struck. I borrowed £30,000 in order to help finance the acquisition of four properties.

How and why?

Whilst researching, I had made some discoveries about the world of property rental in the north of England, and Scunthorpe in particular. As I have mentioned, a good rent for a one-bedroom flat was £50 per week. A two-bed does not command any more money as there is virtually no demand for it. Three-bedroom houses yield about £75 per week but cost almost three times as much to purchase. I went on the hunt for terraced houses that had been converted into two one-bedroom flats, upstairs and downstairs.

Buying a freehold property

Buying a house converted in this manner means that you have bought the freehold to the property, and thus can do anything you like within the boundary walls without seeking first the consent of the freeholder as the lease usually demands. Also you do not need to pay a service charge to anyone, or ground rent. (The service charge is having to pay £50 for the privilege of someone to cut your grass – then again they may not but you still have to pay. Ground rent is a nominal amount paid to the actual person or company that owns the land that the building sits on). As well as these advantages, there is the obvious geographical advantage that one trip in your car means that you will see two tenants, and it would be bloody bad luck if both of them were late with their rent. Finally, because these properties have already been converted into two flats, any new legislation that came into force meant that these houses would be exempt. It's a bit like owning an old classic car that doesn't have seat belts in the back – you don't need to fit them retrospectively.

Borrowing money to get started

Unexpectedly, there were quite a few of said properties around. And I was surprised that these landlords actually wanted to sell (please remember I was still of the opinion that this job called 'landlording' needed nothing more than a spare Friday afternoon to pick up money by the sack load). I found four properties all on the market at a similar price. I wanted to split my money and buy them. That would mean borrowing more money from the bank. This was not difficult as I was putting down such a large deposit on each property the bank was happy to lend. At the time banks were still suffering from the recession and they were not lending as they should. Although the loans that I was taking out were for the purpose of acquiring property, they were not mortgages. Buy-to-let mortgages had not yet emerged so I had to borrow using a commercial loan. At the time I think I was able to get 1.5 per cent above base rate. Base rate then was double what it is today so my repayments were high but still afforded a good return for me.

The fact that I was my father's son did not hurt. My dad was, and still is, very well respected in the town and has always conducted himself impeccably in business. They assumed I was a chip off the old block; they were right. Paying debts, and being a stand up guy, to me means a long life in business. If people know they can trust you, you have their confidence and this will ensure you can ask for help, and at the very least get a foot in the door. Unlike today, bank managers stayed at a branch for many years. They had the power to OK a deal without having to refer it to the branch's head office; these people really did wield the rod of power. It made sense to stay on the bank manager's good side for the obvious reasons, but also to keep him abreast of what you were doing in business did not hurt, in case you needed him in the future.

Integrity and trust in business are vital

Whilst on 'The Apprentice', I found myself in the boardroom on several occasions. To this day I am the only person to have appeared on that show and refused to say who should be nominated to be fired in the boardroom. I just thought it was not the right thing to do. Finger pointing and passing blame onto someone else is a sign of weakness, especially if you are in the position of leader. Furthermore, I was not doing the firing, so if I had nominated someone to be fired, and Sir Alan thought otherwise, there would obviously have been tension between the nominator and nominee the next day. It is not enough to say, 'Well that is part of the show'. Make a decision, stick to it, and then take any resulting heat that arises from it like a man. Pick yourself up, and don't do it again. If you get into the habit of looking to blame someone or something else, you will never learn from your mistakes and you will continue to make those same mistakes until your luck finally runs out.

To this day I am offered jobs by companies that have no idea what I am good at, simply on the strength of how I conducted myself on the show and my integrity, and the knowledge that they can trust me. If I don't buckle under pressure in front of 4,000,000 viewers I can probably cope with most things.

Cracking on

So, I was on the hunt for these four houses all split into two flats each. Each house would yield £110 per week, as I had decided on £55 per week per flat as an appropriate rent. I had also decided that I would try and find properties with sitting tenants. That way I would be assured of a month's rent from each place without the expense of advertising and before I had made my first payment to the bank.

There were certain criteria that I wanted to stick to regarding these properties I was about to buy.

- ◆ They had to all be the same, so all the rents could be justified at £55 per week. That was not only easier for the sums, but also I would become known for this type of property and be able to get savvy with this area of the market.
- ◆ They all had to be in the same part of town so I could get to them easily, preferably walking distance between each one.
- ◆ They all had to have a front and back garden, not coming off the public footpath straight to the front door.
- ◆ They all had to be in the worst part of town. No, you didn't read that wrong. These properties that I was buying were cheap. Therefore I was not going to be able to let them to company directors that drove Jags.

Know your market

My market was the unemployed and people being paid weekly, and these people could only afford this part of town. Had I considered a better area, it would not have made financial sense. Property was so cheap that there was no reason for a person not to buy their own rather than rent. The only people who did rent were ones that were not in a position to buy, such as the unemployed, people with court convictions, those on benefits, and the transient job market where people would come to the town on a contract of a few months and then go. Hence, I knew what I was taking on – or I thought I did.

Back to the house hunt.

I found four houses that fitted all my personally-set criteria. I went round each one with the owner under the pretext that I was the insurance assessor. These properties, although being sold via an agent, were advertised without a board. He didn't want the tenants leaving, afraid of getting a Rigsby-type landlord second time around (even though I always thought he was quite a good land-lord, but a poor ladies' man). Incidentally, these four properties were owned by the same person. I asked him why he wanted to sell, and he told me he was moving to Cyprus. These properties, as is so often the case, had been left to him by his parents in their will.

> You can appreciate that if you approach someone about buying several properties in one transaction, it is more advantageous to the vendor to sell as many as possible to you in that one instant. This will firstly and obviously allow them to feel more secure about the deal, it also means that legal bills will be less and the whole legal process more simplified. Furthermore, the vendor is able to get a better deal from the agent. So be sure that you remember this and use it to your advantage when negotiating price.

I don't really think the vendor was the type to own and run prop-erty, and as a consequence did not even think about leaving the properties to a letting agent while he was abroad. He just wanted shot of them. Knowing his desperation, coupled with the fact that my funds were already in place, I made him a lowish offer. This was not so low that he would have to order his beer as halves instead of pints on the beach of Ayia Napa, neither did I want to get a reputation in a small town of using an advantage and to hell with whomever it affects. Either way he declined my offer and asked only for the asking price. I told him that at asking price I

could only afford three houses – which three would he let me
have? He didn't like the sound of this, obviously he didn't want to
be stuck with a single house whilst thinking about moving abroad,
but I could also see that he didn't know what to suggest, so I spoke
for him: I demanded £2,000 off the asking price of the fourth
house, and wanted to be able to start collecting the rent as of now.
I would give him a goodwill deposit to show good faith and this
would also enable him to start preparing for a life in the sun.
Quite readily he accepted. I asked if he would mind if he introduced me to the tenants and he was happy to do so. He took me
round all the properties and I told all the tenants that I quit my
job as an insurance assessor and I was now a property landlord,
and did anyone watch Rising Damp?

Getting off to a good start

That week I picked up £440 from tenants that were not mine living
in houses that belonged to someone else. In addition, I didn't have
to start paying any money back to the bank for still two months
after that. All the money I was collecting was going into an account
and building nicely. This was all money that I had not expected to
have, of course, nor did I expect to get £2,000 off the asking price. A
bit like my Christmas salesman, who saw me as a desperate soul, I
also acknowledged it in my vendor and used it to my advantage.
Coupled with that the fact that he was going to live a million miles
away, I knew that any resentment he may have harboured toward
me could not be made public all the way from sunny Cyprus.

When we finally exchanged and completed in the same week, I had
almost forgotten that the properties had not been officially mine
all that time. Things had gone really very well. One of the other
provisos had been that the current owner would continue to maintain the properties until we exchanged, so I had no need to keep
any money aside for repairs to the properties as this was not my
responsibility. The only thing I had to worry about was that he may

well have tried to defer doing repairs knowing that he would be out of pocket; fair enough – I would probably have done the same.

The next few weeks were fairly uneventful. The only thing I did was visit each property every Friday night and collect my rent. I would ask the tenants if everything was all right, and go.

> I had no idea about the laws governing tenanted properties and got my basic tuition from the previous landlord. This was at a time when the laws governing tenanted properties did not carry the penalties that they do now if they are broken. I would not advocate that you enter into this field with the lack of knowledge that I had. I am by nature a blagger; you shouldn't want to be.

Each tenant had a rent book, and that, in itself, was a contract, a six month tenancy that kept rolling on each month after the initial 6 month period. In each rent book was written details about what deposit was taken, and I would fill the book in when I picked up the rent for that week. The rent was *always* paid in cash and always paid on a Friday night. If the tenant was not going to be in, by prior agreement he would leave it in a drawer still in the rent book, I would let myself in, sign the book and leave. This is how the previous landlord did things and they suited me fine; I didn't want to make life for the tenants difficult, so stuck with that system. The only possible flaw was that picking up the rent in cash and on a Friday night meant it could not be banked for three days, and the temptation was there to spend it over the weekend.

Keep on top of the maintenance

As a landlord, I actively encouraged tenants to report any problems with their properties as soon as they arose and tried to see to it that they were put right as soon as possible. This made sense to me, as a problem caught early enough meant that it stayed a small problem. If it wasn't reported, it was likely to turn nasty. I am thinking here of a slight leak from the roof – reported early it may only involve slightly adjusting a roof tile. Left to its own devices, the leak could carry on, damp could develop, plaster ceilings could become waterlogged and instead of £30 and up a ladder for 20 minutes the job involves two sets of tradesmen, replastering walls, redecorating, new carpets and a bill for £1,500.

Here is a possible and not unrealistic scenario for you to be aware of. It illustrates how debilitating bills can be on the cash flow: a leaking roof goes undetected. Drops of water land on the first floor ceiling, which is made of plaster. That ceiling, as luck would have it, is the spare room so no one sees it. There is a damp smell in the house and the tenants give their notice. You finally trace the smell just as the ceiling falls in, water everywhere. That room's carpet is ruined and there is a large hole in the ceiling. Furthermore, black soot and 30-year-old dust come falling in also. Before any redecorating can take place or indeed new carpet fitted, the roof needs fixing. Then the room needs to be dried out, about two weeks with heating on full blast. The ceiling re-boarded, then replastered, drying time about a week. Room then redecorated, then new underlay and new carpet after the floorboards have dried out. Then you can advertise that house for letting again. Total time spent on the project about two months, costs about £2,000 not including two months' lost rent. Total time it could have taken: not long. Total amount it should have cost: not much.

Always understand that your properties are yours. You are not only responsible for ensuring that the tenants are happy enough to want to stay, but also for keeping on top of the maintenance. That way between tenants there is less to do, and thus less downtime; critical if you have a mortgage to consider. Repairs can be a killer financially. Very rarely would you be in a position to pay a plumber's £100 call out charge then £30 per hour thereafter. It is precisely for this reason that landlords are in the habit of cutting corners. They do work themselves that should best be left to tradesmen.

Most landlords should easily be able to paint and decorate, unblock drains, fix leaking taps, change locks, garden, bleed radiators and that sort of thing. It is always best to stay away from electrics and gas, otherwise you could be causing more damage than you think. If you cock up the decorating it is nothing more than a little embarrassing, but if you cock up plumbing-in a gas fire that ends up having a blocked flue, you could end up in prison. That is why it is always important to make sure that any small jobs stay small and don't escalate and that you acknowledge what you are capable of doing and what needs expert help.

2

What Have I Done?

The finances

At this point, so far so good. I always thought that the first three to six months were going to be the most enlightening. Of course I had no idea how things were going to go, and it was a bit of a coup that I was earning rent when I shouldn't have been, which made making my first payments to the bank quite easy.

When I discussed the loan with the bank manager I wanted to be able to pay them off early without incurring any penalties. The loan that I took out was over 15 years. I didn't want to get into the habit of paying an extra 10 per cent on each monthly payment, but instead had in my mind that every time I had saved at least £2,000 I would put that towards the loan in one lump sum.

This is all quite reasonable, I hear you say, but don't forget that I was 20 years old at the time. Friends of mine of a similar age were out having a good time, enjoying themselves, and basically spending whatever they earned. Instead I had two jobs, and bank loans hung around my neck like the proverbial albatross. I also had a responsibility to tenants and was really leading the life of someone much older. Still, I made my own bed and hoped that I would start to see the fruits of my labour and risk pay off.

In the first six months, things could not have gone better. None of my tenants put in their notice, I did very few repairs, had a good financial buffer building up (thanks in part to the deal I struck with the former owner) and I was able to do my day job without worrying about my properties.

If you are in the position of having a day job whilst contemplating going into property, I would advise you to keep it. I cannot tell you just how much of a comfort it is to know that there is money coming in while you are getting started. I did not consider that, by working in another field during the day, I was in some way not considering my duties as a landlord seriously. Nor did I feel that I was not applying myself appropriately; rather I considered that what I was doing was sensible and patient.

I was even contemplating expanding because this new property lark was just so easy. There were no rules, or if there were it didn't seem that I needed to know them. The only criteria was that the landlord should be a good bloke and know how to add up multiples of £55. There were times when I actually wanted to find myself something to do.

I had one particular tenant in an upstairs flat, and I called him and asked if everything was OK, or if there was anything that needed to be done. He asked me to pop round for a cup of coffee and a chat. Once there, I asked him how long he had lived there as a tenant, thinking he would say a year or two. I did not expect him to say 17 years!

'What? Why?' I asked. And he actually couldn't really give me a good answer. He was working at British Steel, earning a small fortune. Every night he would be at the Beefeater propping up the bar and he could have bought that flat with three months' wages.

Starting to worry

It was at this point that I started to worry. It occurred to me that if he owned his own property, *he* would be responsible for all the repairs and maintenance to it, and so the only reason he would rent would be so that someone else (muggins) would do and pay for all the work. No wonder the landlord wanted to sell. All these properties were surely on their last legs and they were all filled with long-term tenants aching to get new carpets, new boilers, Sky TV, leather sofas... 'Oh no!' I thought, 'What have I done? No wonder things have been going so well up to now – they are all keeping me sweet before they put in all their requests. I am going to go bankrupt – I don't know what it means but I am sure it happened to Mike Baldwin in Corrie and he was in a right state.'

The only thing I could do was be patient, and wait for an avalanche of requests. I started to think back to the time when I first saw the properties. They all looked OK. Of course I had had a survey done on all of them as I wanted to know about the important points: the roof, any structural cracking and so on. But it has to be said I don't think that I paid much attention to the state of the carpets, or how old the boilers were, and now I come to think of it a couple of places didn't even have boilers, they had those old storage heaters that weighed a ton and immersion heaters for the hot water.

Doing the sums

For the first time in six months I started to do some maths. A new central heating system was £2,000, including fitting. To re-carpet an entire one-bed flat with lino in the kitchen and bathroom about £500; Sky TV they could sing for. All the properties had been sold with the furniture and they were all pretty shaky – goodness knows how much to replace it all. No matter how I looked at it it would be debilitating, my adventure would be at an end before the year was out. OK, I am being ever so slightly melodramatic here, but I was concerned and didn't really know how to proceed. Then, unexpectedly, one of my inherited tenants put his notice in. This was actually good news as far as I was concerned. It meant that this particular fellow thought that it was better to leave than ask for new carpets.

Reality strikes

Once he had gone, I was able to really look closely at what I had bought. And this particular flat was knackered. The carpets were jumbo cord (awful when new, worse when old), the lino in the kitchen and bathroom were so sticky under your feet I could not have imagined that he mopped them once. The oven door was stuck, and when I finally pulled it open an enormous block of gunk fell out. Most of the windows were painted shut and there was damp in the bathroom because of a build up of condensation (because the window was stuck so the steam had no release). What's more I actually gave him back his deposit, all £200 – even if I had kept it, £200 was not going to go very far here and there was no way of proving that the tenant was responsible for all this. He could say it was in this condition when he moved in, and the only witness was in Cyprus. My six months of the easy life was over.

People usually make a big deal about the deposit. If you are the landlord, never consider this to be extra revenue because it isn't. I don't believe that I ever withheld deposit as even if a flat did need the odd bit of DIY here and there, the amount that the tenants hand over very rarely covers it. So keep on the good side of the tenants after they leave and you will have a good reputation in your locality as being fair. It goes without saying that you will take the deposit in the first place, and may indeed need to keep it; all I am saying is don't be in too much of a rush to find trivial faults to justify withholding the bond.

What next?

First I had to take stock of my new situation (of course it wasn't new, but cut me some slack please!). It goes without saying that the better the property, the better class of tenants you will get. But we have already established that I was not looking for a better class of tenant, as I did not believe they existed. So I decided to test the water. I did only the work that was absolutely necessary. First things first, I painted the entire flat… you guessed it, in magnolia. I bet I was one of the first people to fall in love with this colour. I realised that white was very sharp and showed up dirt too easily and yet cream was very expensive to buy (go figure) so this colour Magnolia fitted the bill, as it was warm and could easily be touched up with the colours blending in well. I had to become pretty savvy about paint, as they are not all the same.

A lesson in painting

Interior paint, emulsion, is water based, very easy to apply and you can wash your kit out with running water. It comes in two types, matt and silk. Matt gives a bland, flat finish that cannot really be wiped clean so suits living areas. Silk on the other hand has a shiny hue to it and makes it ideal for bathrooms and kitchens because it *can* be easily wiped, the difference between them, cost wise, is negligible.

Painting tips

◆ Grease and oil cannot be painted over, nor can wax (crayons are wax). Thus, kitchens *must* be washed with a sugar solution before you start to paint, otherwise after all your hard graft, when your paint has dried, all the dirty marks will come through again. (You may then start to use bad language hoping this will fix the problem, it doesn't, but by all means give it a go anyway.)

- All woodwork should be undercoated and glossed. Both these paints are oil based which makes them tough. Always remember to give the surfaces you are about paint a good rub down as the paint will bond better. Recently, new undercoat and gloss paints that are water based have been introduced to the marketplace. Don't be tempted into buying these thinking that your brushes will be easier to clean afterwards as these water-based paints are rubbish. They are extremely thin, do not stand up to constant cleaning, and used as an exterior paint will not last one winter. Stick to the good stuff, buy some white spirit to clean up with, and you won't regret it.

- It makes sense to do all the painting first before any new carpet needs to go down. Prepare the walls with Polyfilla and crack on. It is quite therapeutic once you start. Cutting-in should always be done first, around door frames, windows and skirting boards, then you can roller to your heart's content. If you don't have carpets on the floor by all means make as much mess as you like.

- And finally, if there is a damp patch that has slightly discoloured, paint over it using undercoat. Because it is oil based it will not allow any damp through it, then when the undercoat has dried, you can paint over it with emulsion.

Flooring

Once the painting was done, I ordered the carpet for just the living room. Carpet is pretty much the best type of floor covering that there is for this type of situation. There has been a trend to lay wood flooring and laminate to give a modern feel, and they are both hard-wearing and good heat insulators, but please be aware that in most leases the landlord will not allow this type of flooring to be laid because of the lack of sound-deadening qualities. Even though you may be the freeholder, I would still advise you not to lay this type of flooring because of this problem.

Furthermore, laminate flooring in kitchens and bathrooms is an absolute no no, as the joins between the boards are susceptible to the water and steam that are an inevitable consequence of these rooms, and as such will cause the laminate to lift and the glue from the woodblock flooring to ease so lifting the floor. You have been warned.

Cleaning up

Although the bedroom carpet was just about dead, I refused to give it the last rights, instead I gave it a good vacuuming, and put the double bed over the worst bit, then bought a rug for the rest of the room. All the furniture in the flat, without exception, was for the skip, but after a good clean and a prayer, it was sound. Next on the list were the two lots of lino. The kitchen lino was really just extremely dirty, so lots of hot water and bleach, then mopped till I dropped. With regards to the oven, I didn't even know where to start so I cleaned the hob, shut the oven door and just hoped that my next lot of tenants wouldn't know how to bake anything.

All in all, this took about two weeks of evenings (remember I still had a day job). If this was my main job it would still have taken over a week because paint needs time to dry, and carpets have to be ordered. When all the walls were painted, the carpet down, the furniture cleaned and the lino mopped, I stood back and closed my eyes hoping that when I opened them, the flat would look like Kim and Aggie had spent a week there. Unfortunately, when I opened my eyes, the flat looked like someone had pushed a bed over a dodgy bit of carpet, the cooker needed condemning and the walls were painted to try and mask a horrible state of affairs. Well, it's done now, I thought. Time to put it in the paper and get it let.

Advertising

I had no idea as to the type of person that would actually want a place like this for £55 per week, so I tried to broaden my potential market and included people that were on housing benefit and income support. My phone was red hot. I advertised the flat on a Friday, which was the local paper's property night, and I had viewings all over the weekend. To tell you the truth, I could have let the flat to any one of those that came to view it, but in the end I let it to the one and only person sensible enough to have come to view it with £250 in cash on him. He was on the dole and told me that he was eligible for housing benefit. Enter my foray into the dark abyss that is known as the Housing Benefit Department.

Benefits

The Housing Benefit Department (HBD) is like no other local government department. Some people say that its sole purpose is to deliberately confuse you until either you go insane, or you give up. I didn't go insane, and am not the sort to give up, especially not where my rent is concerned. The HBD is always in arrears by up to ten weeks. All their forms have to be filled in like an American Green Card application form, any mistake and the lot gets sent back, usually after about nine weeks.

One of the problems with this department is that they are not totally privy to all the information about any particular individual, and need the help and resources of other departments to get answers. For example, they will need information from the unemployment office about the state of a claimant because the claimant is not obliged to inform the HBD of a change of circumstance. In fact in many cases claimants deliberately avoid telling the HBD of a change of circumstance for fear of losing their housing benefit, and thus being thrown out of their rented accommodation. They prefer to wait until the HBD find out themselves, then claim ignorance when they are approached with this information. Worse still, the landlord can sometimes be the one to repay the council.

Financial responsibility

Let me explain.

If a tenant is on income support the HBD will pay their rent (they should do, it's their job). The landlord is obviously aware of this. The rent will be sent to the claimant and it is incumbent upon them to give this to the landlord. I see that you are starting to spot a potential hazard here. Because the HBD work 10 weeks in arrears, the claimant then receives a cheque for £550. Some tenants are so overcome at this amount that it makes them go slightly dizzy and abscond. I thought that there had to be something better. And there was. There is a wonderful form called a 'landlord declaration form' that means that all monies for the purpose of rent go straight to the landlord, bypassing the tenant altogether. This was indeed a great form but there was a snag. If there was any money owing to the council because of any skulduggery by the tenant, it would be the landlord's responsibility to repay all the money back to the HBD. As it was the landlord that had received it directly from them, it would then be his/her responsibility to sue the tenant for it back… the tenant that had just absconded.

This landlord declaration was certainly not foolproof, but it was good enough for the time being. I had to be able to trust this system, as in 1990 unemployment was rising and in a northern industrial town this trend was set to continue. I was not resigning myself to only having tenants that were on benefits, but providing I was guaranteed the rent, I was happy to oblige. Furthermore, it was quite astonishing how many landlords would advertise their properties in the local newspaper as 'No DSS'. It dawned on me that this was an obvious gold mine. Council properties were not as abundant as they had been ten years earlier, and so those on benefits had to go to the private sector for housing or Housing Associations. These were not-for-profit organisations who charged less rent, but if the HBD paid the rent in its entirety then as far as the tenant was concerned, it didn't matter what the rent was.

Tenants: the good, the bad and the ugly

In order to be a successful property landlord, you only need to do one thing right, and that is collect your rent.

Everything else you do is merely to facilitate this. And because of this one crucial point, it is essential that you make collecting the rent as easy as possible, and that means getting the right tenant.

I was already starting to realise that property acquisition and letting was not merely a Friday night occupation and to do it properly demanded dedication, especially if your tenants were not BMW-driving stockbrokers who earn a year's wages in one week. This was a tough northern town with tough northern people, but of course when these people came to look round your flat they wouldn't be tough but the most caring, sympathetic tenants that a landlord could ever hope to meet. Once they got the keys, their character somehow changed. The stories I have about the wrong tenant alone could fill this book, and make several episodes of *Panorama*.

Drug users

My particular northern town had not only the problem of high unemployment, but, as with many depressed areas, heroin was rife. The areas that I had just bought in saw prolific use of the drug and people exhibiting all the usual behavioural problems associated with it such as burglary and muggings. I am not without pity for heroin addicts; I know that no one puts a gun to their heads and makes them take the drug, but once they are on it I do believe that society should show some compassion. However I do not believe that compassion should take the form of allowing them to steal my combination boiler, or set fire to my kitchen.

Because heroin addicts to landlords are definitely *persona non grata*, when looking to rent a flat they would often send someone else in their stead. Once that person was successful, the addict would move in, go to the HBD and fill out all the appropriate forms themselves. The original tenant would then be free to go and find another place to live, and before you knew it you had several drug users living in your flat which now contains nothing because all the furniture has been stolen and sold to feed their addiction. All that is left is what looks like a homage to *Trainspotting*. So many parents have seen bright, intelligent sons and daughters go completely off the rails and turn into unrecognisable people once they are hooked on heroin. The only thing I can say here is that no matter how much you want to try and help people with heroin addiction, the best way is to volunteer your services to specialist organisations set up to help them. *Never* try to help by letting property to them.

Now then, onto a lighter note.

Hard prison offenders

To this day, after 16 years of property letting, the best tenant that I ever had was straight out of prison. He had just served 15 years. A friend of mine remarked, 'He must have been a bad bastard to have served 15 years.' Bad or not, he was around 50 years old, 6'4', and kept the flat immaculately. He was a sort of 'man of the world', and had a take on everything. I used to go round just to say hello, we would have a cup of coffee and just chat about nothing in particular. Never once did I mention prison, fearing he may then do another 15 years. He was a tenant for about a year and then he put in his notice. I was flabbergasted. I couldn't believe he would go to another landlord; the HBD were paying his rent so that could not have been an issue. Eventually I discovered that he wanted to move to Grimsby where his son and daughter lived and I suppose he just wanted to be near them. I lost a good bloke, not just a good tenant.

The way in which I got this ex-offender as a tenant was via Humbercare. They were a not-for-profit organisation set up to try and house offenders on leaving prison. Government figures show that people are far less likely to reoffend straight from leaving prison if they have somewhere decent to live on the outside. There was still a lot of risk on the part of the landlord; the only difference was that these tenants had people taking an interest in them and visiting them frequently. There was also the advantage that should anything go wrong I could go to Humbercare for help and they would do their very best to do what they could, trying to keep on the right side of the landlord to guarantee future business.

Exploring different avenues to get tenants was something that I did contrary to the norm. It was usually the rule that people advertised in the property section of the local paper and waited for the phone to ring. Of course I also adopted this system with great success, but the ideal scenario was to have people approach you so you could form a waiting list. This saves the time, money and effort that goes into advertising, and when people come to you from an advert there is no time to get to know them – it's you and your luck.

Young tenants

Youngsters would sometimes come to me for a place to rent, and I tried to avoid letting to them. Usually they would come because of an argument at home, and a couple of weeks later the argument had blown over and they wanted to leave. Furthermore, the HBD declared that 18 year olds were no longer entitled to housing benefit for a one-bedroom flat, suggesting that they didn't need it. They could only secure the rent on a bedsit at £35 per week. They could, of course, take a one-bedroom flat but they would have to make up the difference themselves, and after three weeks they would start to fall into arrears. Without exception, letting to someone under the age of 21 has been a minor disaster. Initially, I would try to get the parents to act as guarantor (so that they would pick up any debt accrued by the son/daughter). Sensible parents would know this was a little spat at home and refuse to act as guarantor; parents that *would* act as guarantor alarmed me as they actually wanted their child out of the house. If that were the case, why would I want them as tenants? So it was 'no' to that as well.

Female tenants

Tricky one this. I don't want to alienate female buyers, yet I have to be honest and this book would not do to be dishonest.

I always had trouble with the fairer sex (as tenants that is, my married life is fine thank you for asking). I remember my mother, of all people, telling me to be mindful when letting property to women. Men are sometimes capable of doing certain jobs about the place without the need to bother the landlord. Although this is going to sound like a sweeping generalisation, women do tend to call on the services and expertise of the landlord much more often – think here about moving wardrobes or unblocking drains.

Furthermore, I experienced difficulties with female tenants because of the men in their lives involving themselves unnecessarily. Dads, brothers and boyfriends would regularly confront me about the amount of rent that their sister, daughter or girlfriend was paying, whether I had the right to pick up rent after 7pm, why the radiator hadn't been bled after almost a week, etc. etc.

So you see, invariably, problems can sometimes arise through no fault of the person themselves, but as a direct consequence of who they are. Fathers, brothers and boyfriends are always more protective of the women in their lives and ergo feel that they should be more involved especially when it is something as potentially tricky as renting out a flat from a guy in a flash suit with a big car.

3

Getting On With It

Once I had let that first flat, to a *fairly* decent tenant, it occurred to me that providing any property was clean, it would let. It also dawned on me that because so many landlords would not take on the DSS, I pretty much had the run of the place. That is not to say that because these tenants were on welfare they would only consider a poorer quality place to live, or that their expectations were set lower than those people working. But it has to be said that when you yourself work hard and then give a proportion of that income to a landlord, you want the best you can afford and the best the landlord can supply. Renters on housing benefit don't pay their own rent, it is paid for by the state, and so landlords are of the view that they will be less inclined to look after the property (my experience tends to back up that theory).

The next few months saw me doing a lot of remedial work to the properties I already had. As tenants left, I had to go through each property as I had done with that first and work my behind off to get them in a state fit for purpose. I also want to make clear that on every occasion I gave back all their deposit to this first lot of tenants. I was sure that a lot of the damage that was caused in the flats was as a direct consequence of neglect by the tenants and not just wear and tear over the term of the tenancy. The deposit taken, however, was so low that it hardly made any difference if I kept it or not. Asking for more deposit was simply not realistic as most tenants would not have been able to lay their hands on any more. But more significantly I knew this to be a small town, and I didn't need word getting around that I penny pinched or that I was not a stand-up guy.

As I have already stated, landlords have to be able to do much of the work themselves. You learn a lot about yourself scrubbing the inside of someone else's toilet, especially when it has not been cleaned for a number of years.

> Paying someone else to clean the toilet is simply idiotic. It is such an awful job, that no one will do it properly apart from you as you have a vested interest in the place (the flat not the toilet), and it will cost you good money NOT to have that job done right. Just breathe through your mouth, think of Carmen Electra (or whoever floats your boat) and just get on with it.

Looking after the properties

Once these particularly nasty jobs were done I was able to stand back, smell the bleach and admire the work. Other things that needed doing, like replacing carpet, were simply outlay – I would never suggest that you fit the carpet yourself. It is a very specialist job, and one wrong cut with the Stanley knife means that the entire piece is ruined. Fitting central heating is obviously an expensive pastime. I had the advantage that I had my financial buffer that had accrued earlier on. I was hoping that I would be able to use this as a deposit on another property, but I had to change tack. I fitted central heating to the first of my properties when vacant. A house split into two one-bedroom flats will have two central heating systems working completely independently of each other. Hence, the price is doubled. Furthermore, it has been known for developers to split houses into two or more flats without the proper consent, and have only one set of utilities coming into the building. This is very tricky to get around when needing two gas pipes in order to supply two boilers. At the time, a combination boiler was about £500 (I only needed a small one, as the flat was only one bed).

> Combination boilers heat as much water as you need as and when you need it. Turning on a hot tap works rather like flicking a switch. It activates the boiler and within seconds your water is piping hot. There is a drawback in that when another hot tap is turned on the water pressure drops considerably; having a shower is fine as long as no one else is washing up. One-bedroom flats occupied by no more than two people are OK to have combination boilers, but for five bed houses with two baths and the prospect of several people using the hot water at any one time you may want to consider other types.

The radiators and fitting the boiler was an extra £1,000. I wanted to find a plumber that I could then start to depend upon for all future work, and this meant that he would not just get the meaty jobs of fitting full heating systems but also be on call-out for Christmas Eve should I require it. I managed to find such a chap. I explained to him that I had a few flats that needed central heating fitting but that financially I would not able to do them all in one go. At the same time I demanded a keen price for all this work, and I guaranteed that all plumbing-related work that I had would go to him. It was a deal. I subsequently went on to use him for 16 years. He was not a one-man band – using this sort is always dangerous when you have several properties to look after. If he is involved in a big job somewhere else, and has other work pending, it is unlikely he will drop everything to turn one of your pilot lights on. This plumber had two main men, and two vans, but also two more plumbers' mates that were able to take care of small jobs. Ideal.

Keeping track of finances

It took me two years to save up enough money to turn my flats into something vaguely resembling a place where people might actually want to live, and pay for the privilege. I could, of course, have gone to my bank and borrowed another few thousand pounds. They would have duly obliged as at this stage I had not missed a single payment and they must have considered that all things were going well – and to a degree they were right.

But I am not one for ever-increasing debt. I didn't get my first (and only) credit card until I was 27 years old. And saving up was something that had been instilled upon me since I was young. I took a year to pay off my first electric guitar when I was 11 years old. It was two pounds a week starting in January 1981, and I finally made the last payment just before Christmas of the same year. To this day, if I haven't got the money I can't afford it. Anyway, I digress. Saving up to buy carpet and heating systems and this and that meant that this new business of mine could support itself in difficult times.

Exapnding my portfolio

It was only at this point that I could reasonably consider expanding my property portfolio. Although financially things were going OK, the amounts of money involved were miniscule. £55 per week is not enough for all the work involved, but the rents could not really be increased. The town had a rental ceiling and that was £55 for a one bed – furthermore the HBD would only pay this amount for their claimants and most of my tenants were claiming benefit. So the only way to earn more from my property was to have more property.

Rent was the only thing I was considering. It was still the early Nineties and capital appreciation was a pipe dream. If anyone had suggested that the properties I was buying would one day be worth double or triple the amount I paid for them, I would have died laughing. The only reason these properties were worth anything at all was because of their ability to produce an income. That income had to be worked for.

So, with a day job to consider, I thought long and hard about buying more property. I still wanted to buy the types of property that I had started with – terraced houses converted in to two one-bedroom flat – as I was starting to become more known in the town as a landlord of this type of property. So I started to save up again, this time for a deposit against, hopefully, two more houses: four more flats.

Rising prices

As I started looking in estate agent windows, I made a bit of a shock discovery. All the types of property that I was after were really quite expensive. I knew that the market had not moved on, so couldn't understand the price difference. It turned out that I had got such a good deal with my first purchase precisely because of the condition of the property, and now that I had spent all that time and money on them they were worth significantly more.

The thought had occurred to me to put them on the market, and make a fast buck, but this flew in the face of what I was trying to achieve – a new career, in readiness for the demise of my current one. I also thought about remortgaging my existing property to fund others, but this meant that I would actually own less of the bricks and mortar and the bank would own more, and I wanted to be debt free, not to acquire more debt! So I did it the old fashioned way, saved up some deposit and borrowed the rest. I now had to borrow more, in light of the current prices, but nevertheless it still represented a good return. The typical prices for two one-bedroom flats were now about £27,500. Let at £55 per week each meant you would get your money back in five years. Still a good deal.

Payment

In business, I have always found that it pays to be a good payer. Cash flow for small firms can be crippling if people are slow to pay bills. I have always used payment to my advantage. When a job is done, I will call the tradesman that night to see how it all went, visit the site and check the work, and ask him there and then how much the bill is. The next day I send a cheque in the post, and ask for a receipt and the invoice he was going to do. If two people need that tradesman in the middle of the night, and I am one of them, who do you think he will work for? And do his very best for?

I have known so many people throughout my life that make a habit of paying companies or tradesmen at the last minute when the court summons is on the way, and I simply do not understand why. It is almost as if they are displaying a sense of power over them. It goes without saying that adopting this approach will mean that you are always on the hunt for tradesmen, and in a small town, word will soon get around about how poor a payer you are. Only the bad tradesmen will want to work for you; the work will be of a poor standard and you will spend much of your life complaining about something you had the power to remedy. A bad reputation, in my opinion, can never be erased; don't try to earn one early in your career.

Getting cocky (a tale of woe)

In my town, there were not too many estate agents and the ones that were there tended to be known for a particular type of property or look after a particular geographical area. The agent that I went to wasn't known in the slightest for terraced housing in the rough part of town, but they were one of the biggest so I thought I could use their expertise about property in general. As it happens they did have one or two houses on their books that were worth a look. The first was nice but simply too dear; it was in too good a condition for me to contemplate. Obviously it had been owner occupied prior to going on to the market. I did not need this level of quality for a rental property and the price hike was down to the quality of fixtures and fittings.

The second house was more like it. When I saw the photo, I guessed the price of the house to within a fiver of the asking price. It was £19,500. However, it was a three-bedroom terraced house and had not been converted into flats. Furthermore, trying to do so would have been awkward because of its layout. This house would have realised about £75, maybe £80, per week, and I would have been safe in the knowledge that the HBD would have paid this amount in its entirety for the right tenant. This means that the property would have to be let in accordance to what the council thinks are a potential tenant's reasonable circumstances.

Important note: The HBD consider that children up to the age of nine can share a bedroom, but that girls can get their own room at seven. So a family of four with two children of the same sex under the age of nine will only get paid housing benefit for a two-bed house (£65 per week) and if they take a larger one, they will have to make up the shortfall themselves.

I also thought that it would not hurt for me to broaden my property types and thus maybe introduce a new type of tenant – families. I went to the estate agent to see about viewing this house.

For some reason, agents always seem to be busy whether they actually are or not, and this one was no different. I think he was implying that it was a buoyant market (in 1993 I don't think so!). I suggested to him that, as he was so busy, could he trust me with the keys and I would give the house the once over? I like to take my time looking at a property as it has to earn me a living so I need to be sure that all is correct. I am not one to second view properties – there should be no need to if you have viewed it correctly first time around. The agent agreed and gave me the keys.

The house was on the market with vacant possession and, luckily for me, in move-in condition. It was not beautiful but everything worked. The decor was OK (the obligatory woodchip was doing what it was supposed to – acting as wallpaper not keeping the house up as is often the case), the kitchen was clean, as was the bathroom, and the toilet was spot on (sigh of relief).

I went home that night thinking about putting in an offer, as I liked the house. The fact that I would only be able to let it as one single entity, as opposed to two flats, did mean a loss in rent, but the fact that I could now attract families meant that the tenants would stay in the property for longer, and so six-month lets could turn into lets lasting several years.

If you are in the position of deciding where and what to buy, remember to take other factors into consideration than just how much it is and how much you will earn. Property that is more suited to family living may mean a slight dip in yield, but your cash flow is more likely to stay constant over a longer period of time. This may well be very important when considering its longer term future.

This house had many positives; it was on a good road and away from the poor areas that I usually bought in, but was still cheap enough to make the figures work. There was a bit of a problem though. This house sale would take about three months to go through, and on top of that by the time I had advertised for tenants, found them, put in the relevant housing benefit claim forms and then received my first rent cheque, nigh on half a year would have passed by.

So I had a brainwave. I would cut myself a second set of keys from the agent's master set (by all means raise your eyebrows). The next day, I offered the asking price on the house (there was no need to haggle as the house was cheap to start with), and I also demanded that the property be taken off the market. I asked if, as the property was vacant, I could start to decorate it before exchange. With all my requests being agreed, I advertised the house in the local paper. I didn't see any harm in doing this. I was purchasing the house, I had permission by the owner to be in the house – who was I hurting?

Tricky tenants

After a week I showed round a couple of pensioners. They loved the house and said that they would take it straight away. They gave me a pretty poor deposit but the fact that they were pensioners was great news as I thought they would see out their days in this house. Furthermore, they would be on housing benefit for the rest of their lives. So handshakes all round. I gave them a rent book, filled out the usual forms, but then hit upon a snag. The worst kind of snag. On filling out the housing benefit forms they wanted the rent to be sent to them and then they would forward it on to me. They obviously didn't know me. I said, 'No Chance'. I told them that I wouldn't do that for the Pope, and I am Catholic. The fact that they were not insistent, however, led me to drop my guard. I handed all the forms in and waited for the cheque to arrive.

As was usually the case I would have had to wait ten weeks, but on calling the council found that they were working much better and that I should have already received the cheque. I told the new Mrs Awkward I hadn't (housing benefit department personnel have a life expectancy of about three months usually because of dealing with the likes of me). Just in case the cheque did mistakenly go to the tenants I thought I had better go to see them. Once there, I found them at home and very genial as usual. 'No, Paul, no cheque here.' I was confused, but it was a Friday so maybe it was still in the post.

Don't forget at this point I still don't actually own the house.

Rent problems

Monday came and still no sign of the cheque, so back to the HBD and to my horror discovered that the cheque was sent to the tenant as *they* had requested. Even though the law had changed to stop this, they had made an exception for these people for undisclosable reasons. Straight to the house. No one home. I opened the door and looked around. No one to be seen. Came back the next day. They were in. In fairly bullish, after the nine o'clock watershed language, I asked them what they were playing at, stealing my rent, and told them not to bother saying it was in the post. They made a fantastic excuse of saying that they had lost their granddaughter and they were behind on paying for the funeral. These sort of excuses are definitely the best because if I don't believe them and say so, I run the risk of being wrong and lose a tenant. If I am right it still means that I am so heartless as to have suggested that they may have lied about something so awful (does that make sense?). They said that they would pay back every penny. I left in a mardy.

Four weeks later, my hands were starting to get all clammy expecting my next cheque. Lo and behold it did not arrive. I rang the HBD only to be told that once again the cheque went to them as asked. This time I had had enough. I went to the house. No one in. I asked a neighbour their whereabouts; apparently they were away for the week. Of course they were – I would be if I had just nicked my landlord's money. Nothing else for it, I got a man with a large white van and put all their goods into my warehouse for safe keeping until they returned. I also did the decent thing and changed all the locks. Then I put a little note on the back door:

> *I called round to see you but you were not there. I assume you have moved away so took the precaution of changing the locks. You can of course have the new keys, just give me a ring. By the way you owe me seven hundred quid.*

Still at this point I don't actually own the house.

Getting stickier

Two weeks later I received a letter from a solicitor suggesting that I had illegally evicted his clients, and that I should make proper reparations. I, of course, did nothing of the sort and told the solicitor to leave me alone (again in after the watershed language, firm but fair I thought considering he was a solicitor). This, I was to discover, was the least of my problems. Another letter landed on my doorstep, this time from the council but not the HBD, this letter came from the fraudulent claims department asking me to come in when I could. I duly obliged the next day. Of course I thought that this case would be about the pensioners making false claims and that the HBD would try to recover the rent cheques from me as was usually the case, but this time I was in the driving seat as I had not actually received any rent.

A door opened and I was asked to enter a small room, not unlike a police cell (apparently). The reason I was there was nothing to do with a false claim put forward by those pesky pensioners, it was about a false claim put in by... *me*. I couldn't believe what I was hearing. I hadn't done anything wrong; everything I did was all above board. OK, I had let the house without telling the owner but that was no concern for the council... was it? Well apparently it was. I had made a small mistake. On the housing benefit forms were various questions pertaining to the property and the tenant, but one form had some questions asking about the landlord.

A question of identity

As was usually the case with me, I owned the property that I was letting, so when asked 'Who is your landlord?' they rightly put 'Paul Torrisi'. Then they asked the landlord his/her relationship with the property, 'Are you agent or owner?' and I put 'owner'. Had I put 'agent' there would have not been an issue, but I had lied by saying that I was the owner. At that point we had still not exchanged contracts and therefore I was not the owner and the fraud department were not happy about it.

I had to really give it my best shot with a very stern-looking man sat by a tape recorder (councils have the power of arrest). I told him that by ticking this box I had acted in error not malice. As he knew, all the other properties that I rented out were actually mine and this was merely an oversight on my part. Furthermore, I *was* actually buying the property and had committed myself to a deposit and had some work done to the house. I was really just getting ahead of myself. I knew that the council worked ten weeks in arrears and that by the time the claim had gone through the house would have been mine; trust the council to get themselves in order when I didn't need them to. Mr Stern believed me, as he should because what he had just been told was indeed the truth.

I left the building feeling pretty lucky as the punishment could have been quite serious, but fortunately I was in the clear. The day then went from bad to worse. I went to my warehouse to find that it had been broken into, and several items stolen. Oddly, the only items that were taken had come from the pensioner's house. Straight away I called the police, and they already knew about it. In fact, the pensioners had told the police that I had taken their items and put them into my warehouse, and it was the police who suggested that they take them back. Thank you very much.

The next day I called my solicitor and told him not to proceed with the purchase of that house. I had a bad feeling about it. I called the owner and apologised. He had no idea that I had let it out (for nothing as it turns out), but I offered to pay all his legal bills and a bit on top to show that I was a stand-up guy. He was happy with that. I learned an awful lot in those few weeks.

4

The Competition

Although I had had a near miss earlier, I was still after more property. I really do learn from my mistakes (sometimes… occasionally). So no more funny business; next time I was going to play it straight. I went to a new estate agent (I couldn't possibly risk going to the same one and suffering all that finger pointing). This agent knew his beans about this type of property and the new breed of landlord that was emerging, trying to take advantage of cheap properties and guaranteed council rents. I saw two properties that fitted the bill. They were both on the same side of the same road and I already owned a property between them. This seemed more than just good fortune.

> Properties that are all within the same locality are definitely worth more to an individual than if they are spaced apart, as there is the opportunity to create one dwelling if they are all together, such as a hotel, bed and breakfast, and so on.

These properties were houses that were separated into one-bedroom flats and they were at the right money: £27,500 each. The agent told me not to bother making an offer as the vendor would not consider it, so I didn't bother trying, and paid the money. I also thought that I would get the key cut again and let the flat out before exchanging on the property. I know that you are holding your heads at this moment but this time I was going to let the flat to a cash tenant (no flies on me). So I did, but I hit a snag.

The vendor decided to visit one of the flats the morning of completion and saw that it was let. The tenant said that he had been there for six weeks. The vendor then went to his solicitor and in rather business-like fashion asked for half of all the rents received from all the flats, working on the premise that they had all been let for six weeks. I split the money and gave another sigh of relief. After completion I knew I had some explaining to do with the actual tenant that saw the then vendor.

I considered saying that the man in question was simply a buffoon and that the tenant should not pay any attention but to let me know if he came round again. But I decided to tell him the truth, and then lost the tenant. The rest of the tenants stayed in place and two even had jobs. Once the other two flats were rented out I had a grand total of 12 flats. I was 23 years old, with a day job learning how to run a garment factory.

A few months went by and things were in good order. People were paying me rent, the council were paying me rent, albeit late, the properties were being looked after and I was learning all the time about the pitfalls of my new profession and trying to avoid them.

It was at about this time that I started to really notice what the other landlords and property people were doing in the town and how they were going about their profession. The best of the rest were really split into two camps: the Asians and the builders.

Asian dominance

In England there is a propensity to bung groups of people together. The word Asian obviously means people from that continent. But if you were to use that term in the USA, you would be referring to the Chinese. We, of course, don't. We mean Pakistanis, Bangladeshis and Indians. Pakistanis and Bangladeshi people are Islamic in their faith (that is why the state of Pakistan was created in 1947, to accommodate the Islamic people that once lived in India). Indians by and large are Hindu. The religion of these peoples play an important part in how they go about business and will become apparent.

One thing that they all have in common though, is that their homeland, compared to Britain, is very, very, poor. So although now it is a standing joke, people from these places will work extremely hard and earn as much as they can. They try to be as efficient as possible and property letting affords that very real possibility. A person can buy a property, let it and run it on evenings and weekends whilst holding down a day job – I should know. Furthermore, one reason that Asian people, first generation especially, liked property letting is that there is no real need to master the language in order to accomplish this, and being first generation, they did not go to school and learn the English language. (When they married, their children – second generation – learned English as a matter of course). Thus the only jobs they could get were not particularly well paid because they needed a good level of English no matter how well skilled they were back in their homeland. So by buying and letting property, they could make ends meet.

Clubbing together

There is another reason why the Asian people were, and still are, very successful at this. When they came to England, as has already been established, they entered into employment at a low level, so in order to climb the housing ladder most people had to be very frugal and save as much deposit as they could in order to borrow the rest from a bank or building society. Unfortunately, Muslim people are not allowed to borrow from organisations charging interest on the loan. So they had to buy in another manner and that was by clubbing together.

Many Islamic families are large in their number and this means that they do not need to turn to outsiders in order to buy property. Each member of the family puts down his/her portion (nearly always equal to the others) and they are able to buy the property outright. Moreover, because they are effectively cash buyers, they can put extra pressure on the vendor to sell at a keener price, as they are not locked in a chain or do not have to wait for funds to come through.

Second generation

Scunthorpe at the time had a large steel mill employing many tens of thousands of people and many Asian men. This was very well paid, and second generation Asian men could command better salaries because they were well schooled. Coupled with their parent's propensity to buy property, they were able to purchase property without the need of help from other family members. As a result they owned these properties outright. They would go to work during the day and either look after their properties at night or, better still, have their parents look after them during the day. Their parents would be happy to do this, as they were by this stage either retired or had given up their poorly-paid jobs in favour of helping their children become successful, or spending more time with new grandchildren.

As is the culture with many Islamic countries, these first generation Asians command great respect from their juniors and it is a sad indictment of our society that we do not have that same respect for our elders. Fathers and grandfathers are always held in high regard by the younger members of this society, to such an extent that in many cases money is sent (by the younger generation) from Britain to Pakistan or Bangladesh in readiness for their retirement so they can afford to buy quality homes in their respective home- lands. This obviously means that not every penny earned in Britain can go towards property acquisition here, so their property has to work for them. My experience with Asian landlords, who subsequently became my friends, showed me much about their life and how they did business.

Landlords that were roughly my age took a great deal of advice from their elders. A lot of it had its grounding from life back in their homelands and was not really applicable in modern Britain, but it would have been unheard of to go against this advice as it would have looked as though the years of experience gleaned from these elders was worthless.

It is predominantly the quality of the rental properties that was called into question. It is fair to say that a landlord letting his flat for £55 per week does not need to offer shagpile carpet and limestone bathrooms. But because of Asian attitudes towards money, and their affinity still with their respective homelands, Asian properties were, in my experience, done up to a very tight budget so they constantly suffered from the obvious consequences of this. They had desperate tenants that would take these properties just until something better came along, which was nearly always anything else. The reason that these properties were in poor quality was two-fold.

1 They thought the tenants did not need anything better as they were always in and out so quickly (work it out).

2 Most of the spare money that they earned was sent back to their homelands to fund building projects and help look after the elderly in that community (and not reinvested). The first generation Asians would always provide the link between themselves and the homeland. Once those second-generation Asians have children and then grandchildren, the link is diluted and they become more westernised and look upon England as their home, not just their *current* home.

The builders

These landlords could not have been more different to the Asian landlords. Whereas the Asians would do their very best to maximise their profit potential (basically by offering as little as possible) builders would not be particularly bothered, it seemed, if the property was let or not. This is down to their attitude towards the property itself and what it meant to them

Looking for a bargain

Builders have a great advantage over us mere mortals in the world of property purchase and letting because they are capable of having all types of building work done at cost price. Buying property in poor condition is something most landlords cannot even contemplate because of the downtime involved in getting the place up to speed. A builder, on the other hand, looks for precisely this type of property. The more rundown the better. It goes without saying that these properties are at the very bottom of the price ladder. There is nothing that is cheaper than a rundown property requiring a lot of work, except perhaps for a property requiring structural work. Again, a good builder worth his salt will know how this can be fixed, but demand that the price reflect the trickiness of the work involved

Making it pay

In the early Nineties, the property market was still very fragile and bricks and mortar had a set worth in different parts of the country. If there was a row of turnkey, four-bedroom Victorian terraces all valued at roughly £75,000, and one went on the market for £50,000, you can bet your bottom dollar that not only would there be a lot of remedial work to do but that whatever builder you called in to do the work he would ask for £25,000 to make sure that there was no money in it for you.

The cost price of the building works involved would probably be nearer £5,000. Thus if a builder bought the house and did the work at cost price the house will stand him in at £55,000 and therefore he does not need the market to move on, nor does he care whether the house then lets or not, because he stands to make £20,000 anyway.

He may be even smarter and take advantage of the tax laws which say that your own house where you live with your family is exempt from any tax, capital gains or income tax. If, after the work has been done to this builder's house, he moves his family in and then lives there, when he sells it he will not have to pay any tax on it. This can happen as often as you like, providing there are no other properties bringing in an income. That is why builders do not like to rent out properties as these are obviously not first residences. They do not need tenants making a mess of things for £55 per week, potentially costing them thousands again getting the house in order for it to be put on the market.

Fixtures and fittings

Either way, the situation created by the builders and the Asians played into my hands very nicely. I also was not going to go mad with the fixtures and fittings, but the places had to be clean. I wanted to be able to stand in a flat and ask myself 'Would I live here?' and answer yes; then there should be no reason why others wouldn't want to. The properties all came fully furnished. By that I mean double bed, wardrobe and chest of drawers in the bedroom. At least a sofa and an armchair in the living room, as well as a coffee table. The kitchen had a cooker, fridge and dining table. Bathrooms usually had a bath and the whole place would be carpeted everywhere except the kitchen and bathrooms which were lino.

Furnished lettings

There are pros and cons to letting property furnished. As far as I was concerned, my properties were easier to let, as my type of tenant really didn't have very much and so were grateful for not having to purchase anything sizeable. Another plus was that if anything was missing when the tenant put in their notice without the need for an inventory, I would know that they had to replace it as it would have been mine. And finally, it is easier to evict a tenant when all they have to do when leaving is pack a bag and walk out of the door. It is a very different story when vans have to be hired along with a team of people to help lug furniture.

The drawback is that you as the landlord have to maintain everything. When the cooker breaks down you have to fix it. But having said that, at least you as the landlord are well aware of the state of your cooker; another person's may be extremely dangerous and end up starting a fire.

> Do not be put off letting fully furnished thinking that it will cost a small fortune to purchase everything.

Some canny buying means you can get a second-hand fridge for £50, and there is nothing much to go wrong with a fridge (when transporting it, if you have to lay it on its side leave it for one hour before switching it on when you put it upright again as the gas in the bottle will have to settle). A gas cooker is a better buy than an electric one. There is *absolutely* nothing to go wrong with a gas one, and again second hand they can be bought for £80. You will have to get it plumbed in by a Corgi-registered plumber but then all will be OK for many years to come. (Quick note: a gas cooker has to be chained to the wall. There is a flame on the hob so the chain stops the cooker from toppling over and starting a fire.)

Sofas and the like have to be fire retardant and second hand suites are at about the £150 mark. Bedroom suites can cost whatever you like but I once bought a wardrobe, chest of drawers and two bed-side tables in the arts and crafts style in the early Nineties from an auction for £4 (they wouldn't deliver it free, though). That same suite now would be £800. I only got really lucky that once, but buying furniture was not a regular pastime. Beds and wardrobes and coffee tables are pretty robust and thus would last a number of years before they were truly ready for furniture heaven.

Since I let all my property fully furnished, there were times when I had to turn away the odd tenant because they had some furniture themselves. Although I had a warehouse, it was really for cookers and fridges that I bought when I saw them going cheap and so would need somewhere to store them. I didn't want to get into the habit of becoming a part-time removal man for my own places.

The property market in this area was still very capable of allowing all of us the opportunity to grow and make a living. The trick was trying to be as efficient as possible. This, of course, meant as little downtime as possible. Downtime is the killer. Weeks going past with no one in your property can be financially crippling and unnecessary.

Keeping tenants

I have already mentioned the importance of finding good tenants: those that look after your property, pay their rent and stay for a long time. I will go one stage further and say that for me I only had to get two out of three right as I knew I would be getting paid my rent. So when you have found your ideal tenant, and by the way you will know when they are not, make sure that you keep them. Do not try to be their mate. A mate can tap you for a couple of quid; your tenants cannot. Your mate can ask you for favours; your tenants cannot. Do you see where this is going? The relationship between you and your tenants is strictly business and cannot get friendly. If it gets friendly it will be you that suffers as you have nothing to gain from this situation. Your attitude towards your tenants and your property should be firm and responsible. Treat your property as you would wish your tenants to treat it.

> When you visit your tenants, take your shoes off when you go in. It is unrealistic to expect your tenants to do so, but it does set a precedent for the sort of standard that you expect from them. Furthermore, they will not take anything for granted when it comes to the returning of their deposit.

Some landlords (not me) were known to give cash bonuses at the end of the year if the properties were in good order, and this gave the tenants the incentive to stay on. Don't get me wrong, I understand this concept, but wouldn't do it on principle. It is a bit like the time bonuses that some factories give their staff simply for not turning up to work late – in other words they get paid extra if they come to work on time. Isn't that what they are supposed to do anyway? Not unlike getting five points on an exam paper just for spelling your own name. No, I don't advocate these sorts of measures. If your tenant sees that he has a good landlord that does what a good landlord is supposed to do and maybe a little more on top, then they will stay, and your relationship with them will be genuine.

A case in point (and yet another tale of woe)

At one point I bought two houses next to each other that were both split into flats, so there were four flats on one block. The tenants knew that they all had the same landlord. Oddly, for me, three of these tenants were working and two of those worked shifts. One flat became empty, and again unusually for me, a prospective tenant came from a newspaper article wearing a suit and carrying bundles of cash. I showed him the flat and he said that to be honest he had seen better, but it wasn't too bad, and that he would take it. He was also on benefit. This was odd as he was obviously loaded. He said that he fixed computers on the side and although it was lucrative work it was very sporadic and officially he was on disability. We shook hands, and the deal was done.

After no more than a week, one of the tenants in this block put in their notice. She was called Jane and lived alone apart from two cats. I am not a big fan of animals in my flats but she was a good tenant and was never going to get a boyfriend in a hurry, so I cut her some slack. I asked what the reason was and she told me that she had had an altercation with the new guy upstairs about playing his music very loud. Immediately I went to see him, and found him to be very pleasant and the flat very clean and tidy. I asked him quite politely about the music situation; he was upset that he had caused the other tenant to come to me about this and it would never happen again. I then went downstairs and gave Jane this bit of news.

All was well again… until next week. She not only put her notice in but another of my tenants was very angry with this new guy for reasons more to do with general behaviour. Upstairs I went again, but this time my new tenant was not the pleasant, jovial fellow of last week. His tone had changed, and he was quite aggressive about the other tenants. He even suggested that there was a clique that he had not fitted into because he was new. This time I cut *him* some slack.

Jane was having none of it and two weeks later she left. She was actually quite scruffy as it turns out – those cats did more damage than I at first thought. As Jane had left, I needed to go round each day to redecorate the newly vacant flat and although the music upstairs was quite loud it was not 'the end of the world' loud. The real problem was what I saw happen next.

I looked out of my window to see two men approaching my building. They were known in the town to be drug users, and the tenant upstairs was so blasé he didn't even show them in. The exchange took place on the doorstep and it was all over in less than thirty seconds. Drug users are trouble enough, but drug dealers can bring a whole new world of trouble. This explained the bundles of cash and the fact the flat was so spick and span: he had the funds to keep it that way. Nothing for it, he had to go.

At the beginning of the next week I went to see him. I am 5'7' (5'8' in the morning); this particular chap about 6'2. Don't get me wrong, he was no Conan the Barbarian, but his reach was longer than mine. I confronted him *mano a mano* as the Mexicans would say, and told him that by Friday night, he would be out. There then followed all the usual bravado from him that I expected, 'I'm not ******* leaving; I'd like to see you try…'. I then left.

As I was going home I realised that I had thrown down the gauntlet. This tenant was obviously a drug dealer, and therefore would probably arm himself with as many people from that fraternity as he could find come Friday night. It also occurred to me that the only thing I had to my advantage was a poster of Bruce Lee in *Enter the Dragon* (you know, the one with him standing there holding those chains above his head after that amazing fight scene) that I had as reference, but that hadn't hung on my wall since I was a teenager. I also knew that come the day of reckoning, if I jumped into a faux karate stance, even if it was a proper one that the Shaolin monks use, he would laugh himself silly and word would get round this small town that I would think I am a Shaolin monk. So, I had to fight fire with fire.

I decided to approach a bloke that I knew. He and four friends came with me to see the tenant that Friday night. They were Glaswegians. As we entered, he was alone. All his gear was packed and ready for off. The flat was immaculate, and he had redecorated (to a very high order as it happens). All that bravado was just that, bravado. I returned his deposit. I also asked him how much it had cost him to redecorate the flat – it was about £200 – so I gave him that as well. This was not an issue about money, or rent, or even a clash of personalities between the two of us. Quite simply it was business. He was costing me. People were leaving my properties because of his behaviour and no matter what else, he was selling heroin from my property. The next day I was in town, and as bad luck would have it, saw him approaching me. Our eyes met, he gave me a wink and said, 'All right Paul?' and carried on walking.

I am of the opinion that he thought I acted the night before as a stand-up guy. I did not rob him of his deposit. I also gave him what he was due because of the decorating in the flat, and so any animosity that he may have thought about harbouring toward me was quickly dispelled. However, it did not hurt that I arrived at the flat with enough genuine muscle to intimidate him and let him know that 5'7' or not, I was to be taken seriously on all levels, even his.

5

The Business of Business

By this stage I was earning more from my property than my day job, and it has to be said that working at being a property landlord required a lot less time than the hours I was devoting to the textile industry. As I was becoming a more accomplished businessman, I started to learn not only about myself but also those around me in the same field. Some people call this psychology, but I don't believe you need to give the study of human beings this grandiose title.

Changing views

The way other people work has always intrigued me. You can learn an awful lot about people by the manner in which they go about their business. I have always been taught that you should 'keep your cards close to your chest'. I suppose this mantra is somewhat out of date in today's 'live flash and brag about your wealth' society. Rolex watches and Porsche Carreras are *de rigueur* for people in their twenties nowadays, whereas twenty years ago it was the privilege of company directors at twice their age. They like to show that they are on the up, that whatever they decided to do, it worked.

Making an impression

But it is just as easy to create the illusion that you are doing better than you actually are. A second-hand Rolex is half the price of a new one, and you can lease a £60,000 car for one year easily enough, without actually committing to buying it and being burdened with the running costs; but what does that say about you?

> When you need to see your bank manager, what impression are you creating? Will he be impressed? Will you get the money you are after? Will he think that you are a safe bet?

Difficult to say really. But I think that bank managers are more impressed with the 'steady Eddie' type, not 'earn it today gone tomorrow' type. Of course I am not one to judge – I am not the one they are trying to impress.

The way people view business has changed markedly. Not too many years ago, a person wishing to set up in business would have to have drawn up a five-year plan. If they were looking to borrow bank money, it was viewed as sensible to have the first two years as loss making since banks do not think that it is feasible to be making any sort of profit within this time frame unless you are buying a going concern (a company that has already been trading for a period and thus, will hopefully already be in to profit). Banks also view this favourably as it assumes that you are not in a hurry to go in to profit and will be unlikely to cut corners and thus says a lot about you as a person.

However, it has to be noted, that you should instil to banks / moneylenders that you are going in to this new venture in order to make money. Otherwise what is the point? You have to imply a certain sense of greed, an ambition to do well financially – that is why you are taking the risk. You will yourself be putting down some capital (deposit) and I dare say that this has been hard earned. Again, lenders look favourably on people who put down as much deposit as they can find. This shows that they themselves have faith in whatever they are about to do. It also shows commitment and they begrudge borrowing any more than they need to because they have such faith in their project – they want as much of the turnover as possible to go into their bank savings account, not to their bank as repayments.

Paying it off

I was no different. But in this case all I could do was save up the deposit and borrow more in order to fund more property acquisition; again the 'old fashioned' way. The new way is different and again it depends on a person's mindset. Because it was important for me to own the bricks and mortar, or at least as much as I could, I would borrow and keep trying to pay off what I already had. Thus when I picked up my rent, less and less of it was going into the bank's coffers.

It is true that you are able to put the interest part of a bank loan against the tax, but any part that is capital repayment (that is to say actually paying off a proportion of the building you have bought) *is* subject to tax.

There was a propensity to purchase property with interest-only mortgages only a few years ago.

In order for this to work the following factors have to be in place:

1 Your rent has to be more than your repayment. You *have* to let you property out and not speculate on the market.
2 The market has to be rising, so at the end of the loan when the bank asks for their money back (you have only paid interest), you have to sell your property for more than you paid for it. This is not really a concern as after, say, 20 years, even at a rise of just the rate of inflation, this will be the case.

But very, very rarely do people actually keep to the term of the loan. Our parents' generation aside, do you know anyone that is coming to the end of a 25-year mortgage that they have had with the same lender or on the same property? No. We just do not live in that sort of world anymore. There is no such thing as a long-term investment in my view. Everybody wants a fast buck. Me included.

Let me pose this question. If you were left £100,000 by a generous uncle in his will, would you want that in one hit, or at £10,000 per year over ten years? Exactly, in one hit. Why is that? Could it be to do with our general lack of faith in businesses nowadays? I suppose this might have started with the Robert Maxwell scandal, where thousands of people lost their pensions because of the greed of one man. Or the mighty American super companies like Enron whose directors are currently serving so many years behind bars that their impressive car collections will all be classics by the time they come out.

Length of investments

I view property as a short-term investment, up to five years. Long-term investments are not part of our society anymore and are impossible to predict. I could not have anything sitting on the back burner for 20 years hoping that that particular ship would come in. It is simply not possible to predict a market coming to fruition in 20 years time.

> It is possible to have a good stab at speculating about a place or a market within five years and no more.

I know that there are people, I suppose with money to burn, that may buy land on the moon, or an area of the Amazonian Rainforest hoping that in their lifetime, or the lifetime of their children, these places will be the next hot spot. If so they can take all the credit for knowing that it would happen all along, even though it was purely guess work not speculation.

The city of Leeds had for many years been pursuing a tram system not unlike the one in Sheffield. This was first put to central government nearly ten years ago. Some people considered that Leeds was too big a city to have this refused and started to buy property on the proposed, or more accurately suspected, tram route. Their idea was that these areas would rise in value because they would become popular with those wishing to commute to the city centre in a decent amount of time without having to resort to purchasing expensive city centre apartments. What happened next? The tram idea was rejected. Those that took a speculative punt on those properties are now back where they started only without even a hope, and sometimes hope is worth something.

However, there is the other side of the coin. The dot-com boom saw the number of millionaires worldwide go stratospheric. People who didn't have anything tangible to sell, became multi-millionaires overnight by selling it. How? What exactly are they selling? I am not asking this rhetorically, I mean it. It does not even make sense to me. Schoolchildren earning more than their parents by dabbling in something or other on the Internet. It just seems that we want short cuts nowadays. We don't want a five-year plan that includes two years of depression and one at break-even. We want success, and we want it now.

Gaining experience

I too wanted success and yes, sooner rather than later would have been helpful, but to be honest, I was happy to look for a new career which by its very nature implies longevity. I wasn't that long out of school and had seen my father spend many, many years in the same profession. I thought not only that this was normal but more secure. The longer you spend in the same line of work the more you get to understand it, and your experience will end up counting for much later on, especially when things turn unexpectedly for the worst.

This is all pretty obvious stuff. An understanding in business is gleaned by understanding your product or service, your competitors, your clients and yourself. I was always comparing myself to others, seeing my weak points and trying to address them. I believe, though, that you can't know everything, or be good at everything. There are times when, as Clint Eastwood said in one of his films, 'A man has to know his limitations.' Clint Eastwood a business guru. Who would have thought it?

Know what you're good at

One of my attributes (notice that I said 'one of'!) is my ability to be able to think and act quickly. I have always been able to see what to do after deliberating for only moments. Even when I have more time to make a decision, I will invariably come back to the conclusion I drew earlier on. If that then turns out to have been the wrong decision, that will be more down to my lack of specific knowledge on the subject rather than lack of due care in making that decision.

Acting quickly

In the business world this can be both a help and a hindrance. People find that it is more advantageous to be able to assess a position roughly and quickly than take their time to get a more accurate result. I am no different. I have attended the Allsop Auctions at the Berkeley Hotel, Knightsbridge on many occasions and the bidding can be frantic. The sight of people raising their hands furiously in increments of £50,000 (the price of a new S Class Mercedes) can seem disconcerting. But of course they have done their maths. They are fully aware of the price point that they are happy to reach in order to attain the yield that they want, and a good businessman and / or a good bidder should not go further than this point.

What happens if the item you are after starts to go for more than you are happy to pay, and is eventually sold to another bidder? You could get up and walk out, grumbling to yourself, or you could look at something else. Of course, you will have absolutely no opportunity to look at the item physically, nor will you have the time to familiarise yourself with it, but if you already know what it is and it is a simple case of crunching the numbers to see if it is worth your while buying it, then the only thing you will need is a brain fast enough to compute the equation and the *cajones* to go for it.

Knowing the value

I have attended second-hand car auctions before, and on one particular occasion I was looking at an Austin Metro for about £1,000. When it came to the bidding the actual car went for £1,500, and I left it as I didn't think that there would be enough of a profit in the vehicle come time to sell. But straight afterwards was a very shiny British racing green MGF on an 'N' plate. This car should have sold at the auction for £11,000, and it had a retail price of £13,000. It was struggling at £8,500, so I offered £9,000 unchallenged, and walked away with it.

My second-hand partner Lee (he isn't second hand of course) suggested that we put the car straight back into the auction, hope for a busier day and make a quick £1,000, but I was thinking big. We had bought the car in November, and soft tops are not all the rage at that time of year. So my plan was to garage it over winter, give it a good clean and wax, then sell it for top book come the spring (£13,000).

The only reason that this offer presented itself to me is that I knew in advance the true worth of that car and I was able to make a decision quickly. While other people in the auction were fumbling for their Prices Guide Index, I had already become its owner.

(As it happens, I ended up begging a dealer to take the car off my hands the following May for £7,000. The bottom had completely fallen out of the market that Christmas and it was costing me too much to have as a trophy. But you get my point.)

Getting an advantage

I knew that Asian landlords were extremely canny and efficient, but also that their properties were rough (sweeping generalisation). I also understood that builders-come landlords had properties that were turnkey with respect to their quality, but that they were not really fussy about them being let. If they were, it absolutely had to be to the right tenant. So to safeguard this, they would ask for an unfeasibly high deposit, alienating most of the potential market. They knew that the only people that could pay it, really would look after their property. Of course these people were very few and far between.

I had to be an amalgam of both. I had to be efficient as I had bills to pay, but I also wanted to provide good-quality housing to ensure longevity in this new-found business. I was looking at this as a new career for me: the start of something possibly for the rest of my life. I couldn't have properties sitting around empty waiting for Mr Right (remember no women), but nor could I give potential tenants treats like a microwave oven or dishwasher just to entice them in. This sort of behaviour merely leads to tenants' expectations growing and demanding landlords to give more, for less. So I wasn't going to go down that road. Sometimes you have to be patient.

Getting jobs done

Where builder landlords had the advantage was that their properties usually, although definitely not always, were of a very high standard ready to be put on to the market. They were also blessed with being in the position of being able to put right most sorts of defects within the property because of their expertise, and as we have already mentioned they can do all this at cost. So knowing how to do certain jobs as part of my landlord repertoire was not merely a time-filling exercise, but vital as a means to getting know my properties inside and out.

> Knowing how much to pay for certain jobs (outside your capabilities) is a massive advantage only really gleaned from experience.

That same experience tells me roughly how much I should pay to remove my tired old kitchen and replace it for a B&Q one that I have already ordered, plus or minus 10 per cent, otherwise you are at the mercy of those doing the work. It is also important to know how to have an edge over what your competition is up to any which way you can.

Working out the competition

I stayed on good terms with local estate agents; finding out who was buying what that might interest me (and hence other landlords), and of course what they were paying. The local paper's property pages were important sources not just for me to advertise my wares but for everyone else advertising theirs. You would see the usual suspects appearing week after week as you got to recognise certain telephone numbers and the wording of certain advertisements.

Ones to be aware of were those adverts that were in the paper perpetually. This not only implied a sense of grandeur on the part of the landlord, but that he had so many properties he needed this regular advertising every week, and also that he was trying to create a waiting list. He can vet tenants without having to commit to letting to them. If he likes them he can undoubtedly keep them in mind for any opportunities that arise sooner rather than later.

Tradesmen

Furthermore, some tradesmen got onto the property bandwagon, investing any spare cash that they might have in bricks and mortar. Call me cynical, but I would try to avoid using tradesmen that had properties of their own. I suppose you could call it a conflict of interest, but I could not believe that I would really be getting the best service possible. These tradesmen would often tell what I could only describe as bordering on idiotic tales of the way in which other people in their profession worked. Believe it or not, I had a plumber once tell me that he knew of another in the same town that actually looked for gas leaks with a lighter. I looked at him with slightly frowned eyes trying to imply that not even an utter buffoon would have believed it. Needless to say, that was the one and only job he did for me. Not because he was an idiot, but because anyone that needed to invent those sorts of stories about their competition was not confident enough in their own ability to get work on the strength of that alone.

Getting friendly

I tried, on more than one occasion, to look at other landlord's properties. What better time to do so than once I had befriended them. Scunthorpe is a small town, and you are bound to bump into another landlord going about their business at some point. Generally landlords, as is human nature, are proud of their properties and so will be quite happy to show them off. A bit like a new mother adoring her ugly baby, landlords with poor properties will not be able to see the squalor.

Properties though, are much of a muchness. A one-bedroom flat is a one-bedroom flat. The difference, for a tenant, will be in the way their landlord looks after their property. As I used to say to my tenants, 'This is my house, but it is your home.' I meant that I would not shirk away from my responsibilities as a landlord but that I expected my tenants to behave towards the property and their neighbours as if it were theirs. I am not sure that it was taken as anything more than lip service, but I meant it in good faith.

Financial aptitude

This new world that I had entered required me to be tough. It was not Neverland. I absolutely did my best to try and make sure that I was not going to be 'had' when it came to any aspect of landlording, especially money. I was working far too hard to throw my money away. This was no place to be complacent, and at the time there were no 'How To' manuals to help me. I learned the old fashioned way, by making as few mistakes as I could get away with.

To tell the truth, I have never advocated learning from your mistakes. It is always best to try to avoid learning from your mistakes as this means making errors to start with. In property this could mean tens of thousands of pounds-worth of mistakes. I think it is better that you simply do not make mistakes. Before you think that this is all very well but a little difficult to achieve in reality, I beg to differ. I mentioned earlier that in order to do this right, you only need to get your rent paid. People will happily pay you the rent that you demand providing you have everything in place in order to achieve this.

- ◆ **Research**: The right property, in the correct area, bought at the right price so that it is all financially worth your trouble.
- ◆ **Character**: The right attitude towards tradesmen and the need for repairs to be done correctly.
- ◆ **Knowledge**: At least a basic understanding of business and accounting.
- ◆ **Good manners**: A respect for your tenants to be viewed as human beings, not merely objects that pay a set amount each week.

◆ **Awareness**: An appreciation for the business that you have entered, and the desire to learn as much as you can from it. This includes knowing your competition and dealing with them, irrespective of their size, type or capability.

These are not principles that I gleaned from anyone or anywhere, but they have been fundamental precepts, and ensured longevity for me in a business that all too often takes more scalps than the media tend to report.

6

A Bit of Luck

The reason I went in to property rental in the first place was that I had been made aware that the business that I was currently in did not really have much future. The textile industry, as with most industry in Britain at the time, was not healthy. Recently as a company we had been ticking along, but nothing more. The company that we made for were the Burton Group, and as with most high street retailers at the time, they were getting the majority of their products made offshore, understanding that domestic companies simply couldn't compete with the Bulgarians or Polish producing pairs of trousers for 75p.

Making connections

Our company was a highly regarded CMT factory (Cut, Make and Trim), and as such enjoyed better work than the majority in Britain. This still did not mean that we could afford to be complacent, or that any storm on the horizon would neatly avoid us. In 1995, the year before I actually took over the company, we were approached by a young designer not long out of college, Brian. He had a job designing for a Huddersfield based clothing company, themselves not too big. After one or two small orders of 100 or 200 garments from local stores, he started to look for factories. My father was not interested. Nothing personal but that it was down to order size. Let me explain: our factory produced 6,000-7,000 garments per week. It takes time to set up machines and downtime in a factory is crippling, so orders of a couple of hundred were simply not worth our while, as they would cost us to produce them.

Taking a chance

I have to say that I got on very well with Brian and pressured my father to allow me to do his orders with a small line set up for him. It did not quite go to plan, and I had to tell Brian that we could only do his work as and when we could fit it in. The situation was not ideal for him, and I would have understood if he had gone elsewhere, but he was intelligent enough to realise that we were a well-respected company and this kudos would hold him in good stead when approaching bigger potential customers. A deal was struck, and we were on our way.

There were some teething problems in the initial orders. He was new to this business and it was up to my father and I to explain how we wanted dockets to come to us, how much notice we needed for material to come in and how much we wanted to do the work. I told Brian that we would be charging him extra for the privilege of these small dockets and he understood.

Responding quickly

After about six months things were going OK and he and I became good friends (not so good that he got discount though). Then one evening at about 10pm he called me at home. He had had a meeting with a company and needed me to cut and make a sample for him super fast. This meant I had to go to the factory to get it cut there and then. Cutting samples is not an easy job and requires patience. That night I had to call my sample machinist, again at home, asking if she would mind my dropping this sample to her first thing the next morning (Saturday) for her to make that day. I would then spend Sunday checking the garment for measurements, trimming it of excess thread, pressing it and bagging it.

Monday morning came and at 7am Brian was already at the factory door as arranged to pick up the garment without even time for a cup of tea. He was on his way to Leicester where this company's headquarters are. He had a pre-arranged meeting with their head buyer for ladies casual wear that morning. He left the sample with her then went off to Paris for the Paris fashion show.

Later that day I received a telephone call from this company asking if I knew where Brian was. As it transpires they were complaining about the fit of the garment. I couldn't believe this to be the case so I informed the buyer, with a straight face, that Brian and I were partners: he was the designer and I the manufacturer, and if she would give me two hours I could be with her to help with her problem. Fine. I told my dad I had to go out for the afternoon, and I went off to Leicester.

Dealing with any situation

On arriving at this mega building, I was suitably intimidated, and the reception desk was raised several feet so that you had to look up to speak to the person manning it. With a cricked neck I asked for the senior ladies-wear buyer and went to see her. Once at the correct department I sought her out and tried to look into the problem.

'The thing is Paul, your size 12 garment is tight in some areas and loose in others,' she began.

'Have you tried it on your size 12 model?' I replied.

'Of course', she said somewhat accusingly, as if she didn't know her own job.

'Can I see it on her?' I asked, being as polite as possible of course, as not only was she the senior buyer, but this was not my gig.

At that, she asked for it to be put on their size 12 model. When I saw the garment on her, I had to agree with the buyer's first sentiments. I asked if I could have a minute alone with the buyer. The model left and I explained to the buyer that her model looked to be over 40 years old, and that a 40-year-old woman does not have a 20-year-old shape (no matter what they reckon). Moreover, this company catered for younger women. The buyer's assistant looked about 25 and a size 10. I asked the buyer to get her assistant to put on the 10; it looked fantastic, and the buyer acknowledged it. We chatted for about ten minutes about the clothing trade, blah, blah, then I left for home.

At the end of the week, Brian rang and thanked me for doing what I did. It paid off. That company was Next, and he and I were asked to make the Next Capri pant, that was all the rage in 1996 and 1997, in three colours.

I cannot remember just how many tens of thousands of garments that order ended up being. It was wonderful news not just because of the order's size, but also as the Burton Group had seriously downsized their British manufacturing operation for that year and orders fell by half. So what initially started out as a small line for a small company turned out to be our major breadwinner for two years and kept the factory going at a time when others were struggling severely.

This anecdote is important in the great scheme of things regarding all aspects of my professional life. Not only did this order mean that I was happy and safe in employment for at least two more years without having to stretch myself by acquiring more property, but the manner in which I dealt with the Next problem showed an already fairly bullish young man that as long as I put my mind to it, I was capable of dealing with any situation single handed, without the need for help, guidance or assistance of any kind from anyone.

Coping alone

This little coup, however, was a double-edged sword. My father had told me that I would be dealing with Brian and his work. Now that this had turned into an enormous task, things did not alter. I was still the one that was looking after the order, and my father thought that now would be a good time for him to relax a little. In 1996 he decided to retire. Because of this, 1996 and 1997 didn't see me do very much apropos property acquisition. What it did mean was that whereas before I was working for a textile company and letting out properties, now I was *running* a textile company with all the responsibility that demands, as well as renting out properties. Furthermore, I had just acquired four more flats to add to my portfolio.

I was not under any misconception though, about the state of the clothing trade. I knew full well that although we were doing all right Jack, the domestic market was suffering. This order, albeit massive, was still only delaying the inevitable. I am not trying to sound fatalistic, or even defeatist, but I was being a realist (that is a lot of *ists*), and the fact that I had landed a good order did not change anything.

Too much to handle

Look at it this way, if you're not blessed with God-given good looks, and you just happen to land a dream date that is not too fussy, that doesn't make you all things to all women does it? I was simply not in a position to carry on growing my property portfolio because I am a hands-on person, and would want to continue dealing with my properties in this manner. Relationships that I had worked hard to forge with the council, with Humbercare and with long-standing tenants needed nurturing. Giving the impression that I had disappeared off the face of the planet was not a good way to go. Moreover, I did not want to exhibit the attitude that my property was not as important to me and my future than my other business. By spending more time at the factory I may have given this impression, especially as I had not had the time to deal with all aspects of my portfolio as I had once done, including the less than pleasant jobs like rodding drains and washing carpets.

As it was things were going to be difficult, as I would have to change the way in which I operated. I would have to deal with a lot more situations at night, after work, or at the weekends, rather than being able to dash out and take care of something quickly as before when I did not have too many factory responsibilities on my shoulders.

A changing climate

Those two years saw me concentrate on what I had. This was a blessing in disguise, as it meant that I was able to consolidate my position, pay off the small bank loans that I had outstanding, and become liquid. The flip side to this was that I was not growing, but was conscious that I could not take my eye off the ball. I knew that I would come back to the property market. I also knew that this period was merely a comma in my property sentence, not a full stop. So it was vital for me to continue to keep abreast of the local property market especially the area in which I was starting to specialise.

A new government

In 1997 things were starting to change outside the world of textiles and property letting. New Labour had just been voted into office, and whilst I am fairly apolitical, in my opinion the Labour Party have never really been the friend of the businessman, even less the private property landlord. This being the case, I thought it prudent that I see out 1997 as quietly as possible, vis-à-vis buying more property, not just because of my extra workload at the factory but also because the political climate was about to change and I wanted to see in which direction I should go next.

The Labour Party's trade union history meant that many people, myself included, thought that they would help the factories here in Britain by imposing taxes on goods made offshore, to encourage large companies to start to get their products made here again. After all, Made in Britain was a label that meant high quality the world over, our only problem was competitiveness. Unfortunately, the government did nothing to remedy the situation. In fact they made it worse by introducing the minimum wage.

This meant that people at the lower end of the wage scale got paid a set amount by law. Although great in theory, the problem now was that Britain was even less competitive against the rest of the world. This country was being steered toward a new type of manufacture.

A new type of business

This new type of manufacturing was tailored towards a quick turn-around that could not be delivered by companies in China or Malaysia, and was heavily reliant on the skill of its workforce not the ability of the machines it utilised. Companies such as ours that employed around 100 people had to make a choice about whether it was able to sustain itself by taking on much smaller dockets and turning those dockets around quickly.

The problem was that I would have to shed 75 per cent of my staff. Furthermore, our factory was approximately 11,000 sq feet and thus would be extremely inefficient to run with so few people. It would still need the heating and lighting to work at the capacity required for 100 people not 25. Business rates and the mainte-nance of the building would also be unchanged.

I did not want to make any decision until as late as possible. This company had been in existence since the Seventies and I did not want to jeopardise it by making a decision I may not need to. I even recruited my father again to bring out his big black book with telephone numbers and contacts from the world of textiles and garment manufacture from 25 years in the business. He was trying to drum up business and I was cutting dockets and running the factory as best I could.

On virtually a daily basis we would get telephone calls from other factories asking to share our work. This was akin to asking a starving squirrel to share an acorn. There was simply not enough to go round, aside from the fact that factories were really not supposed to split their work with others as the quality of the work could not be assured. Those calling us knew this, so they must really have been desperate to have even suggested it.

Stretching the work

Towards the end of 1997 I had started to send staff home early for the Christmas break. The Next orders were finished and they too had started to get their garments made offshore in Morocco. It had crossed my mind to take on certain work that would lose money just to keep the factory going, hoping to weather the storm, but this was not a storm… this was the end that had been predicted a decade earlier. I suppose it is not unlike a person who is ill with a terminal disease; you know that the end is coming, you knew it was coming all along, but you still can't believe it when it finally arrives.

Keeping the factory open

We started to operate a rota system of bringing in different members of staff on different days to allow people the opportunity to earn a few more pounds than just minimum wage. At this time of year this was even more important than usual. Some dockets started to come in to be cut in the new year. All was not lost. As long as we could we would keep the factory open and it would be business as usual until the last minute.

Christmas came and went and we started to cut the dockets that had come in before Christmas. I also did deals with smaller companies and started buying my own cloth. This is extremely high risk, but desperate times require desperate measures. As it happens it paid off and I was not stuck with fabric and garments. I made calls to the large retailers that we had worked for over the years, knowing that they had received countless calls of the same nature by countless other factories all in the same boat.

At the beginning of 1998 things continued to look bleak – in fact they looked worse than they had done before Christmas. Maybe it was because we were now at the beginning of a new year, a time when one looks forward to what could happen through the year with optimism. This time, however, things were different, and I will admit I had no idea what to do.

My father suggested I go away for a week because of all the stress of all that was going on. He would look after the factory while I was away, so I went to Ireland. It was freezing cold and threw it down with rain every day, so now I had problems with the business *and* I was wet.

Decision time

I came back feeling no different to when I left, as the problems that I had left behind had not miraculously disappeared. But my father had drummed up some work while I was away, and we had work at least until Easter and maybe some repeat orders a while after. Suddenly things did not look so bleak. We started to cut the work and more dockets started to come in. Now I was fairly sure that 1998 would see us still trading. Yes, we had to drop our prices, change our system of production and let some people go, but we were alive. We had work.

It was at this point that I knew I had to put my eggs into my other basket. The last few months at the factory were just too close for my liking. I needed the security that my property afforded me, and I needed to grow my portfolio whilst I still wanted to stay within the area of the market that had sustained me for eight years. I was happy and comfortable with it and I didn't need to learn any new tricks at this stage. I was not being blinkered; it was not that I didn't want to explore other aspects of the property market, it is just that now was not the time to start looking at other markets. The Euro would not be in circulation for another two years, the American dollar was still strong, no one had spotted Florida's potential yet and London was still a bit of a speculative punt, so you will forgive me if I stuck with what I knew, at least for the time being.

7

Politics and the Winds of Change

1998, for me at least, started in April. The beginning had seen me take stock of my working life and wonder in which direction I should proceed. That decision was really made for me by what had transpired before Christmas 1997. Although in 1998, things were looking up I was not happy living hand to mouth, especially when my property lettings were doing so very well. Furthermore, the factory was heavily reliant on others giving me the work and it is difficult to be proactive in this situation. There is nothing I can do if a retailer is determined to get their product made offshore because it is so much cheaper.

At least with my property business I really could be proactive. There were so many ways to drum up business, and to keep tenants loyal – stopping them from even contemplating moving.

Hand on heart, apart from all the usual trouble that one would associate with the lettings business, for eight years financially things always went to plan... by and large. It would be a tragedy to back the wrong horse now. In the couple of years that I was working hard at the factory I had taken my eye off the ball somewhat. I had told myself that I wouldn't, but I had.

My particular market hadn't really changed all that much, property prices had stayed fairly flat, tenants were still readily available, but the change came in the form of a new breed of landlord, and this new type of landlord was to be the worst of the lot, although they probably thought of themselves as the best.

By now, the country was on the up. The new government had been in power for almost a year. They were in the wonderful position, as all new goverments are, of being able to claim the credit for anything that was going right, but able to shift the blame away from them and onto the shoulders of the previous government for anything that went pear shaped.

Don't forget I am still apolitical.

From about 1995 onwards, the country was coming out of recession. Things were looking up for the county as a whole. Bank interest rates were coming down as was the rate of inflation. This was symptomatic of the world as a whole, I am not suggesting that it was unique to John Major's policy strategy alone, but I will say that by the time the 1997 election came around, the country was definitely on the up. The only thing that was missing was the 'feel good factor' that John Major and the Conservatives craved. The Labour Party victory in that election was an inevitable consequence of people simply having Tory fatigue. The government had done no more wrong than they had previously, it is simply that voters were starting to get Tory fatigue. That is why in our next election the Labour Party will lose; policy aside, people will just want a change. We have had a Labour government for 10 years (at the time of writing) and a change of leadership will not mean a change in political leaning, merely a new mouthpiece for the same policies.

Irrespective of who is in power, we as individuals have it within us to make our own livelihoods and create our own destiny. Sure, one party might make the top tax band 40 per cent and another 35 per cent but the latter will tax its people somewhere else to regain that lost income. The Treasury is an enormous beast with a seemingly insatiable appetite. It constantly needs feeding. So it is the government's first job to feed it.

The *raison d'etre* of any business is to make money. It will do this by providing a service, or producing goods. It has to have good customer relations, be competitive and so on, but ultimately it has to make more than it spends. Central government is no different. What policies it subjects onto its citizens do not matter one jot in the great scheme of things, but that is not to say that we should not care and leave everything to our accountants and solicitors.

> Remember: knowledge is power. But too much knowledge and your mind is full of information that you don't necessarily need. It ends up acting as a fog, stopping you from making quick decisions clearly. So learn what you need to learn and then go about your business as best you can.

The new breed of landlord

As I mentioned earlier, as a consequence of the country being on the up, and people's outlooks being more optimistic, a new animal had entered the lion's cage. People had been stung by what had happened in the recession of the late Eighties and early Nineties. They had not been comfortable in investing in properties since then, but now things were starting to change. Furthermore, the lower end of the housing scale did not seem to be much of a risk. The properties that concerned me were some of the cheapest in England, and even if it all went wrong, the actual amount lost would not have been so significant that it would lead you to ruin. This new breed of landlord was your average, everyday, working Joe.

The new investors

They had no idea about property or what it meant to be a landlord. They were civil servants, plumbers, IT specialists, those with small businesses and so on. The one thing that they did have in common was that they were all cash rich. They had money, and they wanted a return. Bank rates were falling and savings accounts were not as wholesome as they had been (if you were fortunate enough to have been able to put anything in one that is).

These new landlords bought anything that they could afford and simply let it out. They bought property that was turnkey, as it meant less for them to do. They did not have the time to work on these properties nor did they really have any inclination to. Remember, all they were looking for was a better return on their investment than was offered by the bank; they were not looking to get their hands dirty.

By purchasing properties that were in such good decorative order, they assumed that they would be able to command a better rent, and get a better class of tenant that would look after their new acquisition. This was devastating news for us landlords that already had all the grey hairs we needed. It was bad enough having to compete with this new breed of landlord but we were then going to have to deal with a new breed of tenant – the ones we all dreaded – the demanding ones.

When these new landlords arrived their first port of call, after the estate agents, was the rough end of town. They could not believe that three-bedroom houses could be bought for a little over £20,000 and let for £80 per week, representing a yield of nearly 21 per cent. This was giving them double what the banks could offer in the way of savings and that was not even taking into account the possibility (for it was still only that) of the properties appreciating in value.

Increasing prices

I am not going to say that the arrival of these new property investors came like an avalanche, but it was significant. Initially, they purchased properties that were sold by owner occupiers. These were typically in a far better state of repair than those acquired by landlords. Consequently they cost more, but although significant in percentage terms, in actual pounds and pence it only really represented £3,000–£5,000. They, of course, assumed that this price differential could be offset by asking for higher rent, so were quite prepared to pay the extra.

It is easy to see why these investors behaved in this manner. They had not understood that these properties should only be viewed as cash cows, and not as pretty little ornaments sitting on your granny's shelf. They did not know the market. They did not know their potential clientele. Those that wanted this type of accommodation, in this sort of order, were not likely to go to this part of town to find it.

The winners in all this were the owner occupiers. For several years they had been reduced to selling their properties for no more money than landlords were prepared to pay. This part of town was now rent-ville. The community feeling was leaving the area. There was a time when sons and daughters had bought their houses next to mum and dad's, and families lived within walking distance of each other. Not so now. But these investors had at least offered those wanting to leave, the opportunity to get a proper price. Not only for their house, but some of the cost back for the work and effort that they had put in to make it better than just habitable (as was customary for property landlords). So at least someone was happy.

Enter the estate agents

Once these investors had purchased their properties they would usually leave it up to agents to let them, and it is really only at this point that estate agents saw any financial sense in going into the lettings market. Previous landlords were hands on and had no need for a third party to do some of the work for them, especially not at 15 per cent. However, with this new wave of business coming the way of the agents it just seemed like an opportunity too good to miss. The complete service all rolled into one: sell the property, charge a fee, advertise for a tenant, charge another fee, get it let, charge another fee, pick up the rent, charge another fee and finally the *coup de grâce*, any repairs that need doing, charge a fee on top of the quoted figure as set by the tradesman.

Still these investors came by the bucketload. However, because they were cash buyers, and had no real desire to become property landlords (remember all they wanted was more than 10 per cent return on their money, coupled with the easy life) they would usually only be in a position to buy one, maybe two properties at a time. So if they had a property that was not let, they were earning nothing. Nada. Zero. Zilch. Serious landlords (I think I can call myself serious now) had a portfolio of properties that meant that all their eggs were not just in that one basket, so they were never caught short.

Initially things went quite well for the new investor. It goes without saying that cash purchases go through a lot more quickly than ones requiring any kind of borrowing. They could also, of course, put some leverage on the vendor for a good price, as they were not caught up in a chain. As the purchase went through they would take some advice from the agents (who were not really fit to give it, but what the hey) about the lettings market, and then proceed with them. They would then be free to go home and really forget about the whole thing until the rent cheques started to land on their doorstep, minus 15 per cent. Of course this is a not a bad idea, if it goes to plan, and why shouldn't it?

- They were purchasing property in the correct area for renting it out.
- The quality of the properties to let were of a superior standard than that offered by the current crop of landlords.
- They were using an official agent that (supposedly) knew his beans and could advise on any potential pitfalls.
- They were only seeking market rent plus a little more, reflecting the standard of the décor and fixtures and fittings within.

This all seemed par for the course and things went off without a hitch. The properties did get let eventually. I say 'eventually', because lettings agents cannot move as fast as an owner or sole trader can. Furthermore, many potential tenants can only view the properties at times to suit them, not necessarily to suit the agent. And the new investor does not want to be bothered with showing people round as this sort of defeats the whole purpose of easy investment with no hassles. Thus it was incumbent on the agent to adapt or lose the tenant.

Once the tenant was in the property they were quite happy there. If they had rented previously they would have seen a marked difference in the quality of the property versus anything else in the rental market at that time. (I dare say these tenants may indeed have had some jealous friends renting in the same neighbourhood.) It is only when things started to go wrong that cracks appeared in the new investors' game plan.

What went wrong?

Agents would always, as is human nature, try and make life easy for themselves. This included letting the property to the least troublesome type of tenant. Bear in mind that by this stage I had eight years of getting to know the right and wrong tenant; these agents were just starting to find this out. They looked for people that were working in jobs that paid monthly… no chance, as I already knew.

So they lowered their expectations and looked for those that brought a regular pay cheque, weekly. They were happy with that, and started to get up to speed on landlord tenant law, and the most efficient way of running the whole operation. They would take the deposit and first month's rent, set up a standing order and that was that.

Although in the contract of tenancy there would be a clause saying that the tenant should not withhold access to the lettings agent or property owner, providing they have been given sufficient notice, very rarely were inspections carried out. I, on the other hand, physically went to each property and picked up my rent, so I was always able to talk to the tenants about problems that they may have noticed about the property or changes in their own circumstances. This could be a change of work patterns, a new love interest that may have wished to move in, or indeed a loss of job, in which case I was still able to accommodate them as I took tenants that were on benefits.

Too short-sighted

Tenants, of course, are always very quick to point out defects in where they are living. So I was able to deal with them promptly. As for those tenants that were receiving benefit and whom I didn't need to visit, I would still make a point of going to see them for precisely this reason and deal with any change of circumstance immediately. Letting agents did not have the time to do this. Nor really was it encouraged by their superiors as it would have meant time being unproductive, time which they could spend on the phone back at the office drumming up business. So the agents that were employed by these new investors were really only able to offer the service of 'finder' and no more, but they charged for everything else. It soon became apparent for the agents that they were really not geared up for this type of lettings market.

The money pit

Tenants would leave the properties usually in a fairly poor state. That was not really due to neglect, but it is amazing how tired a property can look after two people have lived there, smoking 20 cigarettes each a day, having friends round and not really looking after it as though it were their own. At the very least the whole place would need redecorating, a job anyone can do if they want to; these owners didn't want to. The property would need a good and thorough clean, including carpets shampooed, hard floors mopped and cookers and ovens cleaned. All in all this was not cheap, nor does it take into account any financial hit due to repairs that the owner would also suffer. There is also the downtime to consider, the time when these properties have to stand empty while the work is carried out, and no money is coming in.

Rather like my first six months being a nice and easy entry into the property world, so it was with this new breed of investor. After their honeymoon period they had to readjust their expectations of what was achievable in the property market and how much they would be prepared to finance it.

Slow to respond

The main fault was that of the lettings agent. They simply couldn't compete with the likes of me. I was able to deal with virtually any situation within minutes if need be. Furthermore, I *wanted* to deal with matters urgently. These were my properties – I didn't want anything happening to them. I worked hard to be able to buy them and I was certainly not going to let anything or anyone distract me from looking after them and earning an income.

Problems mount up

Agents, on the other hand, had lots of far easier jobs on their plate. And this new market still only contributed a relatively small amount in revenue for the agents. At this stage they were *bona fide* estate agents that were offering a lettings service, rather than a dedicated lettings agency who knew all the ins and outs of this new world. Imagine the scenario that was described in Chapter 4: my drug dealer tenant. Is it reasonable to think that an agent would have gone to the lengths that I did in order to deal with this problem? Sure, they may have tried to do something about the situation, but I am fairly sure that another way would have meant months of insecurity for the owner as well as those tenants nearby that were putting in their notice and moving on. Had any of these investors come to me for advice on this area of the property market, I would have advised them to keep their money in a savings account and sleep easy at night.

Now that these investors had seen the light, they also became aware that workers in factories or retail staff that were being paid weekly did not always stay long in work. This meant that they had to contemplate taking on tenants that were on benefits. A decision not to be taken lightly. Official lettings agents were not happy about dealing with tenants that were on benefits. It became a necessity to understand housing benefit law and become savvy with the department as a whole, the way it operated, and understand all the relevant forms that required meticulous filling in.

Certain things started to happen.

A glut of properties

A glut of properties found themselves back on the market, being sold by those that once expected an easy life. Some were on the market at a substantially reduced figure and were consequently snapped up by landlords. It was a bit like watching vultures at a carcass; landlords were all looking for the best bits (I had the odd one or two myself).

Some properties were on the market at pretty much what the owner had paid, only now they were not being sold by proud owner occupiers at a premium because of their quality, but by investors burned by their experiences over the last year; the state of the properties would reflect that.

They saw no advantage in spending the odd £1,000 here or there getting the property up to speed, hoping to entice another naïve investor looking to enter this 'gold mine'. As a result, they were asking top prices for properties that fell well below the standard. The longer these properties stood on the market empty, the more they required money spending on them.

Facing the benefit market

Lettings agents *had* to become familiar with all things pertaining to housing benefit. Many tenants were on benefits and to refuse to deal with them would have meant disassociating themselves from at least half the potential rental market. Furthermore, new investors that did not wish to sell, and who had become more realistic in their expectations of their properties and tenants, were *forcing* letting agents to take on those on benefits, realising that they had to salvage something from the situation. They knew that putting their property on the market would have meant that theirs would have sat for sale along with a million others, all exactly the same.

Sitting empty

I cannot tell you for how many years 'For Sale' boards were put up and properties sat empty. The boards would finally wear completely away before the owner thought about doing anything about their situation. Estate agents did not push these properties as the state of repairs inside and out usually put off most buyers.

I remember viewing one house with a female estate agent. What I saw as I walked into the kitchen made me suggest to this pretty young lady in a nice two piece navy suit and shiny black shoes, not to come in. I didn't think she needed to see its utterly revolting condition. To my regret I had seen it all before; I was fairly sure she hadn't. Thus there the houses sat. The owners had resigned themselves to having made a financial mistake, but the sum involved didn't mean financial ruin for them, and as a result it was a hit that they could stand.

Becoming hands on

Finally some investors started to become more hands on – letting the properties themselves and dealing with the tenants. This is, in my opinion, the best way. Property investment and in particular property letting is not just invest your money and get your return. To do things properly there has to be some involvement on the part of the investor. Otherwise why bother with property? Why not invest in numbers on a sheet? For a risk-free investment, the only way is to save with a bank or government gilt-edge shares. With anything else there is an element of risk. Although playing the markets requires an element of risk, it is nothing more physical than opening the 'pink paper' to see how you have done that day. Property investment is real; it is tangible.

Involving oneself in the rental market means becoming educated about it in all aspects, and requires commitment. This new investor simply didn't do any homework about the market they were getting into. They simply saw what they thought was an opportunity with no adverse consequences.

This period in the late Nineties was also marked by other changes brought about, in part, because of the effects of new investors that were entering the property market. This had an effect on the way we viewed property as a whole.

North Lincolnshire was not reflecting the domestic property market as a whole, nor was it indicative of the country, but it was my little slice of what was going on, and as such it was important that I didn't take my finger off the pulse again.

8

Exasperated Landlords

Housing benefit problems

I may have given the impression that if a landlord and tenant on housing benefit fill out forms correctly, and wait their allotted time, everything will be fine (thieving pensioners aside). This is not quite true. As so many tenants were claiming benefits of one description or another I ended up becoming a familiar face within certain departments at the DSS. I was not alone. As I mentioned earlier, the Housing Benefit Department (HBD) worked 10 weeks in arrears. It is also true that they were sometimes as behind as 13 weeks. Thirteen weeks is an awfully long time to wait for your rent, and I know of no business where payment is this delayed; property letting should be no different.

All sorts of new measures were supposedly brought in by the local authority to try and improve this situation. Most landlords were of the opinion that this was merely lip service designed to imply that this matter was being treated as importantly as it should. I didn't for one minute believe it.

So much can happen within 13 weeks. The HBD could find a fault with the claim after 12 weeks and send it back to the tenant, only to discover that they had left the accommodation. In this situation the landlord would not get paid one penny, even though they were due hundreds of pounds. This was a severe blow indeed, as they would not find out about this problem until the council notified the landlord several weeks after that.

Many landlords were starting to find other holes in the system too. While in the early to mid-Nineties property letting was fairly new and thus every day was an adventure, now it was no longer an adventure. I, for one, wanted to understand this business inside and out. I wanted to be right on the button, finger on the pulse. I wanted to be made aware of any problems very early on; this has always been my mantra. Day one, ten years earlier I wanted people to let me know of any problems so that they could be put right straight away without leaving them to fester and become gangrenous.

Survival

My attitude had definitely changed. Without the safety net of the factory to see me through tough times, I had to make sure that my property business was all that it could be and more. I was a very different animal. I was not going to tolerate any BS from anyone, including local authorities implementing new legislation on almost a weekly basis in order to make life for the private landlord even more difficult than it already was. New measures included the DSS office not being open every weekday as it had been, but rather only open once a week to the public. Any queries could be sent via an e-mail address that never seemed to work, or a phone that never seemed to be answered.

Tenants' changing position

Tenants had been at the mercy of their landlords long enough it seemed. It had been the case that you either liked your rented accommodation or you didn't; either way you still stayed put. Furthermore, at the time landlords did not really have the weight of the council on their shoulders, needling them to put right any problems that had been reported by the tenant, but things were starting to change.

A (sensible) tenant would usually go to their landlord first regarding any physical problem vis-à-vis their rented accommodation, the landlord should then put it right. But obviously not everyone was like me, or the builder landlords. So time went by, and now tenants were actively being encouraged to report any problems to the council as a new body had been set up to weed out this type of landlord. The council wanted to deal with only decent landlords that knew about tenant law, used proper rental contracts and kept their properties in a good state of repair.

Changes in legislation

Recently, there had been a spate of tenants falling ill, and in some cases dying, because of carbon monoxide poisoning. This was due to flues on back boilers becoming blocked, and the toxic gases not being able to escape. In these cases landlords were being taken to court by the local authority, and could be found guilty on the charge of manslaughter, which carried a maximum term of 15 years in prison. More legislation meant that landlords had to have gas and electrical appliances checked by NIC EIC-registered electricians and Corgi-registered gas fitters. The cost of all these certifications was paid for by the landlord and severely ate into their profits. There was no opportunity for them to raise the rent; the town would not stand it and the council would not pay it.

Overload

So, as you might expect, there were a lot of fairly miserable landlords around at this time. It was as if everything was against them.

- The heroin issue that first started in the Eighties, but reached its zenith a decade later, and all the associated problems that brought about;
- Newcomers to the foray of property letting in the form of the new investor;
- Enormous lead times the HBD had self-imposed and the obvious problems this posed;

◆ A bucketload of legislation that needed extra work, time and
expense on the part of the landlord.

We had had enough. But what could be done? The local authority
would not speak to landlords on an individual basis because it
was just too time-consuming, and they were not as yet bringing
out leaflets to try and help property owners that were letting to
those on housing benefit or otherwise. It was as if the landlord
was now the *persona non grata*. Something had to be done.

The North Lincolnshire Landlord Association

By this time I had got to know many other landlords and some of
the new breed of property investor. We would regularly meet at the
Conroy Hotel, owned by Tony (you guessed it) Conroy, and grumble about the state of affairs facing us. To start with, a few of us
would meet unofficially and exchange stories about problem tenants that we should all watch out for, and any new bits of
legislation that would be coming into force.

Getting started

This little band of men tended to be the same group week in week
out. It dawned on me that we should try and form an official body
that spoke with one voice and could approach the local authority as
one entity. Any information gleaned from the local authority could
then be passed on to members either via meetings or a newsletter.
The council would *have* to take notice of us then, and not simply
sweep us under the carpet as they had just started to do.

We discussed how this body would work, who would be in it and
if the council would indeed recognise us. Would we be privy to
private council meetings that may involve legislation pertaining to
private landlords?

We worked out that between us we must have known at least
30 per cent of all the landlords in the town, who would account

for at least 60 per cent of all the property. The system we adopted was that we would have a subcommittee of six people and that whoever was chairman would surrender their right to vote on matters. We would try and put the word out about the committee, hoping to encourage other landlords to join, without having to press-gang them into doing so.

It might be necessary to pay some sort of fee, as we kept drinking Tony's coffee and eating as many bacon sandwiches as we could, but there were also costs of leafleting and other expenditure which had to be taken into account. As it turned out, we discovered that there was a National Landlord Association and it would be a real coup if we could become affiliated to that – then we really would have some weight behind us. Thus, the hunt was on for the six members of the subcommittee.

Forming the subcommitteee

The six couldn't just be people in the same boat with some property that they let. We wanted each person to bring something unique to the table if possible – more than just the usual bitching about the current state of affairs (we could all do that!). It was a given that I would be in the six, as it was my idea; Tony, as it was his place that we met in; and my dad, just because he was my dad. We therefore needed another three, and we found them.

Gerald Denton had recently bought a house in multiple occupation (he regretted it five minutes later), and had been in business for many years. He was a very trustworthy gentleman who was known to all of us, and we knew he would easily fit in the role of treasurer. He was semi-retired, which meant that he was able to attend meetings without too much notice, and he was also able to keep on top of his job as treasurer properly without rushing his work due to other commitments.

Number five came in the form of Steve. I approached him one morning after learning that he owned a bed and breakfast. A friend of mine from London worked for a record company and sometimes laid on gigs in the north. He asked me to find a place to put up a band so that they could then go on to Hull for the gig. Steve had such a place, and on securing a few rooms for this band I got to realise that he may well be the sort of chap we could use on the subcommittee. I told him about it and he was very willing. Again he was not happy about the state of affairs in the property market, and owning a bed and breakfast brought its own headaches which were further exacerbated by new legislation.

I thought very hard before putting him forward to the others, not because he owned a B and B, but because if I continued to give him business, I would have been able to use him as an ally. Let me explain: the subcommittee would consist of six people – only five of whom could vote. My father and I would always vote on matters together and thus we would only need one other person to vote with us to have the motion carried. I felt sure that he would be an asset to the committee, however, so I put his name forward. One of his attributes was the fact that he had a different type of property to the rest of us; he was also young enough to be able to be involved in this committee for many years to come. Deal done. Onto number six. We found a real asset. He had worked for the Housing Benefit Department, (believe it or not) for many years, and had taken early retirement. At that time he was working part time helping his wife do something but wanted to do something a little more official and significant. He was the unknown quantity of the group. None of us had ever met him, even in his housing benefit days, and he had approached us to see if he could be of any assistance as he had spent so much time working for the council. But given his CV, we really didn't care whether he was a potential serial killer; he was privy to all sorts to information that we could only have dreamed about acquiring. He was in. All six good men, present, willing and able.

Recruiting members

Now that we were armed and dangerous came the business of recruiting. We couldn't very well go to our local authority demanding that we be taken seriously as there were only six of us. So we tried to recruit by word of mouth. We had decided that £10 per year would be a sufficient membership fee. This would enable members to know what was going on apropos of local property within the geographical perimeter of the county of North Lincolnshire. We talked to other landlords and within a month had recruited over 30 people, owning a total of 300 properties.

Making plans

Meetings were held at Tony's place (sounds very New York Mafia but was actually his hotel in the town) on a Sunday evening at 7.30pm after Mass (most of the subcommittee, myself and dad included, were Catholic). We started by drawing up a blacklist of problem tenants, making sure that no one inadvertently got them. We also discussed good tradesmen, taking ideas from people who had been satisfied with work done by certain individuals. We contacted these tradesmen and asked if they wanted to work for our new group at a discount. The *quid pro quo* was that there would be an abundance of work. If there was an issue with regards to payment or quality of work it could be dealt with in-house without the need for the small claims court; rather we would act as a family and try to resolve the matter.

This all started to work. I won't say that things went to plan, as initially there was no plan. All we wanted to do was be united with like-minded people. If there could be any advantages along the way, like discounted tradesmen, or knowledge of the property market gleaned from others in a more official manner, then all well and good.

Increasing in size

Our friend, number six had been doing some extra work, and discovered that there was indeed an official body that we could belong to providing certain systems were in place. Better than that, one of their spokespeople was coming down that month to talk to us all about the current lettings climate and difficulties vis-à-vis new legislation and the like, as well as the possibility of joining the national body.

We told all our new members about this Mr Big coming and asked them to pass the word around, hoping to recruit many more landlords on the night. That evening I am sure Tony had never made so much coffee – he had to recruit his wife to help (he is an equal opportunities employer). We welcomed a further 20 landlords that evening, who would have been impressed that we had this spokesperson from the official nation landlord body.

Our group was now 40 strong, all paid up and raring to go. Within two months we had everything in place to ensure that entry into the national body was smooth as possible. Known as the North Lincolnshire Landlord Association, it still operates today (without one of its founding fathers of course, me).

Ploughing on

Now that we, as landlords, had the backing of this new organisation, we were indeed able to speak to official government bodies about anything and everything to do with bricks and mortar and tenancies. This gave me the feeling of optimism that I needed. I was not long out of a bitter relationship with the textile manufacturing world and had also seen many people get their fingers burned by underestimating the complexities of the property market, so although I was mindful of the pitfalls facing anyone in this field, I also wanted to actively pursue it because of the success that I had had during the Nineties. So it was time for expansion.

Expanding my portfolio

I had been looking at some property to buy at the time when the new property investors were putting a sack load of properties back on the market. I believe I described it as vultures at a carcass. I am afraid to say that I was one of those vultures, and I tried to use this glut of properties newly on the market to my advantage.

I wanted to become more efficient in the way that I ran my business. Apart from one particular house, all my properties were located within three interconnected roads. I had one particular house that was located away from the others and was one of those that I had bought for a song. My idea was to sell it and purchase others in the areas that I was more familiar with. The advantage was that I would be able to sell it for what I paid, and then buy property that was newly on the market closer to my area at a similar price. Believe it or not, it worked. I sold the house that was divided into two flats and bought another three-bedroom terraced house, and two other flats all within walking distance of each other.

I managed to sell my Mary Street house for £19,700. I bought a downstairs flat on Buckingham Street for £7,000 and an upstairs flat on Digby Street for £8,500. They were both one-bedroom flats, leasehold and in very good condition. So good, in fact, that I was able to rent them both out as soon as I had the keys (no need for any naughtiness). The downstairs flat I let to a young lady and the upstairs flat that was literally only round the corner I let to a man of about 50 years old who was on long-term income support.

An unusual tenant

The three-bedroom house I bought from the hospital trust and was very different from the types of property that I usually ran. Not just because it was a three-bed house, but because it came with a sitting tenant that had been there for 50 years. William had rented the house in the Fifties from the hospital trust and simply never moved. He was married at the time although now was widowed. His daughter lived right opposite along with her family and they were all really quite happy.

Picking up the rent from old Bill was a new experience also. He was a huge cricket fan, and in the summertime I would go to his house after I had visited all my other properties to pick up my rent. I would sit down, he would offer me a brandy and a cigar and we would watch the play, light permitting. It was all very civilised. Bill was old school and would only drink Three Star Reserve Cognac. Whether the cigars were hand rolled on virgin's thighs or not I couldn't tell, but I ended up looking forward to Bill's Friday night experience, even if it was only to pick up £16.

Making an offer

This house though was not in the best condition and that was reflected in the price that I paid for it – £5,400. Really it needed totally gutting. All the windows, without exception, were rotten, the plumbing was all lead pipe, the carpets looked more like Rab C. Nesbitt's string vest and there was no central heating. The house was stuck in a Fifties' time warp as all the furniture, kitchen and bathroom included, had not been altered since then. The house did not even have an indoor loo. No matter though, for I had a plan. The rent Bill was paying was £16 per week. It was a fixed rate due to the type of tenancy that he had. So my plan was to approach him with the idea that I do the house up for him, completely at my expense: new central heating, new windows, bathroom and so on. During all the work he would live in another place that I had on the same road so he could still be close to his daughter and her family. Then, when the work was finished he would move back in.

Miscalculating

The only stipulation was that I would call in an independent rent assessor after all the works to reassess the rent, which I hoped would be more like £75 per week. But if this was too much I would let him stay in the flat at £55. Everyone's a winner, I thought. But he didn't think so, and asked if he could just put up with the house as it was and pay the same rent. I did not know why anyone would want to stay in that house in that condition, but it simply was not an issue for Bill. So there I left it.

It was not the best use of £5,400, especially only getting £16 per week. That rent I could consider to be net though rather than gross, as I would not have to consider advertising costs, repair costs or even insurance costs. Bill was not young but certainly not old either, and had 20 years left in him at least. Twenty years, I thought, of £16 per week. This was really the first time that I had miscalculated on property. I had my plan worked out in my head before I bought the house, without even considering that it may not work and that I would be stuck with a property yielding around 15 per cent. In today's market many people would settle for that but I was looking at something bigger, more akin to 33 per cent.

Number crunching

I'll show you. The house cost me £5,400. To get it up to speed would cost in the region of £6,600: central heating £1,500, new kitchen and new bathroom £1,500 each, carpets £1,000, new wiring £500, new plumbing £600. I would decorate myself. This means the house would stand me in at £12,000. The new rent would be adjudicated at £75 per week and annually that comes in at just under £4,000. That means my money back in three years, or equates to a yield of 33 per cent. All well and good as long as the tenant says yes… which he didn't. So that plan unfortunately bit the bullet, and I was back to smoking cigars and drinking brandy while watching the cricket. Still not too bad, all things considered.

Bill passed away only two years after I bought the property. He died of a heart attack. Not even 70 years old – the brandy and cigars finally got him. So in the end I got my vacant possession house but not in the manner that I would have wanted it. To this day I have been searching for another cigar and brandy tenant who watches the cricket, it was a great way to end a stressful week. After Bill died, I left the house as it was. A builder saw it and made me an offer in its current state. I decided to take it and pass all that trouble and dust onto someone that was used to it. R.I.P. Bill.

9

Taking Stock, Having a Moan, and Moving On

At this point I was able to take stock of my portfolio in its entirety and able to see what was glaring me in the face. I was paying exactly the same amount for property now as I had done nearly ten years earlier. The property market had simply not moved on. Capital appreciation was only something that was happening in London and the big cities, certainly not in Scunthorpe.

There were opportunities to buy property at lower than market prices but these needed work doing to them, 'fixer uppers' as the Americans would say, and this simply was not my area of expertise (nor did I wish it to be). I was starting to contemplate the possibility of buying further afield, and even exploring a new avenue.

Extra responsibilities

Property letting in my town was starting to become even harder work. I have talked already about why, and although the new landlord association was helping in a big way, that brought its own extra work in the form of attending our own meetings and council meetings designed to help bridge the gap between them and us. There was also more literature to read. Because I was now a full-time property landlord, I found that it made sense to carry out more work myself rather than get tradesmen in who would charge for the privilege.

The last ten years had taught me an awful lot about the property letting business. I consider myself fortunate that I dealt with property at the lower end of the market, for I had to learn quickly. I am sure that I am not being politically incorrect by suggesting that those on income support in Britain's depressed areas, or indeed those habitually taking heroin, are at the lower end of the market, not only in housing but also in society. I faced difficulties on a regular basis, with tenants trying to divert their rent cheques so that they would receive them directly, bypassing me as their landlord. Or arriving at properties that had been vacant for no more than a few days to find that squatters had broken in and were trying to take possession. In ten years of property rental in this small town I had suffered eight arson attacks and – without exaggerating – over 100 break-ins. I had my brand new BMW stolen and destroyed and my next nearly stolen.

Making a change

The fact that after ten years these properties were still valued at almost exactly the same amount as I had paid for them left me feeling that this business was really only about the rent and that nothing else could be eked out of it. I simply couldn't lie in bed with an empty property safe in the knowledge that it was appreciating by £1,000 per week anyway so what was the rush? This was a hands-on job, and not only my hands but the rest of me also was looking for a change. Moaning over.

This prospect of expanding further afield had always been lurking at the back of my mind. I suppose the opportunity had never really presented itself, or that I had not been really in a position to do anything about it because of circumstances relating to the factory, or problems that were arising with new legislation.

Furthermore, I had not really had the time to see past the end of my nose for at least two years. At the beginning of 1998 I was faced with the factory crisis, and towards the end of that year I was starting to experience a harder letting environment due to the demands of more savvy tenants. At the same time local authorities had started introducing measures that had landlords doing more mandatory work to keep trading in the residential lettings market. This required knowledge on the part of the landlord as well as finances. There was also the time I invested in helping to create the North Lincolnshire Landlord Association, which was not inconsiderable. So it was about halfway into 1999 that I was able to look in another direction and explore other facets of the property market.

Spotting new growth

As I said, capital appreciation was really only the preserve of large cities. As the country was coming out of recession, business optimism was growing and companies were expanding again and recruiting. These companies were traditionally based in the larger urban areas and new graduates, sometimes under pressure from parents, would forgo their almost obligatory year off after university and go straight into work. Recently graduated students seeking employment in large cities were obviously not new, but it was becoming more prevalent and in larger numbers. New parts of the country were seeing unprecedented growth, including northern towns and cities, and I started to look in these areas. They were areas that would afford me the opportunity to buy property that was undervalued and hence has the potential to appreciate.

What was I looking for and how would I know if I found it?

To start with I had to concentrate my efforts on a specific area. I couldn't cast my net too wide otherwise I would not be able to understand fully the specifics of that locality. I was also able to use a tool that had not been available to me previously: the Internet.

I already had an idea of where I wanted to start. I had for some time now been going to Leeds on a regular basis to clothes shop on a weekend. The opening of the new Harvey Nichols store in the Nineties suggested it was a better place for me to go than Manchester; again a good place to shop but another hour's drive further away.

> I do believe that it is best to start your property search with some-where that you have knowledge of. It does not have to be your home town, but having some familiarity with the area will at least mean that you will be able to not only get around more quickly, but also be able to come to some conclusions more quickly than if the area was totally alien to you.

Because of this, I started to look at Leeds (Yorkshire not Kent).

Leeds

Leeds is a city. It has a university and a cathedral, and is a good size geographically. The only area that I knew was the city centre because of its shopping and cafés. I was not even contemplating buying there as I am still not totally convinced about city centre living and what it actually affords those who live there. So I wanted to look in the residential areas of the city.

I had no idea where to start so I used a bit of logic and looked on a map. I saw that the south of Leeds was spread either on or very close to the M1 and the M62 with the M621 road coming off it. No one would want to live this close to motorways. Because of this reason and the fact that it was once a site for heavy industry, I discounted the area as somewhere that wouldn't give a good return within a reasonable amount of time. It is important to remember that 'transport links' are all too often banded about without people being really fully aware of the specifics behind the term or what it means for them.

Transport links

Transport links to a Londoner means the tube. This is because virtually everyone who lives in London works in London. At the time of writing, the average salary for a non-manual working man in London is £42,000 per annum. The average salary for the same job in the rest of the county is £27,000. It would therefore be bordering on barmy to live somewhere expensive and earn a low wage. The tube is also the most convenient way of getting about in London, even if at times it is hot, smelly and dense. There is no need to worry about traffic jams so people want to be near them, and rightly so.

Commuters wanting to take advantage of the salary hike given to those working in London, without the desire to live there, will try to live as close to London as possible whilst still enjoying the benefits of less populated areas. Surrey, Kent and to a lesser degree Berkshire, have an ever-swelling population working in London. Transport links to these are the M4 for those in Berkshire, the M20 / M26 for those in Kent and those in Surrey travel on any of the link roads that hit the M25 at any point between Leatherhead and Oxted. It also goes without saying that all these areas have trains that go into any of the major stations in London: Charing Cross, Victoria and London Bridge as well as others. I have journeyed on many of these services and, as an example, from Tadworth to Charing Cross took only 35 minutes and cost £5 return. So transport links here mean outside London going in.

South Leeds

The south side of Leeds, close to the motorway, serves no benefit to those living there as the motorway will only take them out, not in to Leeds to work. However Wakefield, for example, is a different matter. It is a commuter town that is slowly but surely being swallowed up by Leeds. Living near the motorway here would mean access to Leeds within a much shorter time. It would also negate the need to traverse the town in order to hit the motorway, shaving a further half an hour from the journey time twice a day. Ergo, it would be beneficial to live near to the motorway, whether you worked in Leeds or not. Come selling time this area would be promoted to those that did work in Leeds, and that advantage would be realised financially, i.e. people would pay extra for the privilege.

So no to the south of Leeds.

West Leeds

Next I looked at the west of the town. This area had one big disadvantage that no other part suffered from… it bordered Bradford. Bradford was as powerful a town as Leeds 100 years ago, but it has not enjoyed the same investment as Leeds since the Sixties and Seventies. The result is that great swathes of the area were left to ruin.

Why is it then that Bradford, as close as it is to Leeds, has not enjoyed the same prosperity? One reason could certainly be that Leeds has benefited from a strong Jewish community. Jewish communities have tended to put down strong roots wherever they settle and then plough back their wealth into that community. Leeds of course also had a large textile industry until very recently and the city benefited from the wealth accumulated from that. Money attracts money and new niche businesses started to spring up to cater for this new breed of wealthy businessman, of which there were plenty, and their numbers were rising.

Bradford was different. We have already discussed how Asian communities – many of whom are first generation Asian people setting up home in Bradford – certainly create wealth, but that wealth is distributed more widely. Because of their strong family ties with those still living overseas much of what they earned was sent home to ensure a better standard of living for their perhaps elderly relatives. This will change of course as new generations within the

Asian communities expand their own families here. Meanwhile the result of this cultural and economic drive for Bradford is that it has not received the same inward investment as its sister Leeds. Prices in West Leeds, because of its proximity to Bradford, have remained more in line with Bradford.

East Leeds

East Leeds suffered from a similar fate to south Leeds. There we are, that was nice and quick.

North Leeds

Finally, north Leeds.

The best TV cop shows are the ones where the cop (my favourite was Columbo), would always get their villain because of a hunch – nothing concrete, just a feeling. Well I get similar feelings in certain areas of towns and cities that suggest the area may be worth a closer look. Once I got on the central road in Leeds I started to pay more attention to the area the further north I was going.

The first thing I noticed was the greenery. It is not just young families that like parks and open spaces, but also young men quoting Byron to their lady friends whilst courting, or maybe quoting 50 Cent; either way we all like a bit of parkland to stop the monotony of concrete. North Leeds has this in abundance. Furthermore, access out via the north means that places like York, Harrogate and Wetherby are a 20-minute car ride away. Bus routes into the city centre for shopping are thorough and frequent and it was starting to appear that this area had it all. Small pockets of stores and cafés give a village feel and a genuine village know-everyone atmosphere. Parts of north Leeds, like Oakwood, feel very similar to Kew in Surrey. Both are similar in their proximity to their respective city centres, both are green and leafy and both are accordingly expensive. Roundhay, Weetwood and Alwoodley were all the same. It was now up to me to start to look at the property prices of this area, as I had decided that this was it: I had found Valhalla.

Investigating the area you have chosen

Before approaching an agent, I wanted to become an expert in the new area. I reckoned that to become an expert in the whole district of north Leeds would take longer than usual for me, so I gave myself two days instead of one. I went Internet mad for 48 hours solid.

The advantages of getting to know areas before going to an agent are three-fold:

1 You will not be completely at their mercy, and will be less likely to pick up a property that has been on their books forever as you will know in advance that the back garden borders a mainline railway route bound for Kings Cross.

2 You can be aware of anything coming in the future that may have a positive or negative effect on the area. I am thinking here about anything ranging from local laws being passed to allow rock bands to play on a site right in front of your house, to a brownfield site that has been given the go-ahead to be turned into a nature reserve with no possibility to build residential property, and so on.

3 Agents do not work for the buyer, but the seller. Their commission comes from the money gained from the sale of the vendor's house. The more money the property sells for, the more they can get; they do not want to give it away. So it is important for you to get to know the value of property in any given area. There will always be 'chancers' that try it on. These people stick an extra few quid on top so that if they get an offer, it will be easier for the vendor to accept without actually getting less than he/she originally wanted. This has the effect of artificially increasing prices in an area. You do not want to be the sucker that falls for that one, or even worse the sucker that started that whole trend.

Online

The Internet is indeed a wonderful tool, but it does require patience and a methodical mind, neither of which I happen to possess. In 1999, the Internet was not the tool that it is today. It was slow because of the dial-up connection. It was also used as a last resort by property companies because not everyone had a computer at home. I was finding properties that read for sale on the agent's website, but were in fact sold, and had been for months. Usually websites are outsourced by companies who would have so much work on that there was simply a backlog. Times have changed of course, and most sensible companies realise just how powerful this medium is.

Being methodical

When using the Internet I found that it was necessary to have an order in which to approach my work for this particular project. It wasn't sensible just to trawl through web page after web page until I found pretty property that was cheap. So I tried, at first, to compare apples with apples and look at similar properties north, south, east and west of the city. My theories mentioned earlier about these regions were spot on. I would take a type of property that I knew I would be able to find in all parts of the city, in this case a three-bedroom Victorian terrace house with no parking front or back. This could be the standard bearer, and I would be able to see which areas were not only dearer but also by how much.

Analysing the market

My next thought was to go back in time and try to find out the approximate cost of these properties one year earlier. This would demonstrate to me which areas were rising more quickly. Once I found out this information I looked into these areas to see if there was anything glaringly obvious that would suggest to me that further rises were possible, and indeed probable. Moreover, it could indicate reasons as to why they were increasing faster than the other areas to start with.

Appropriately enough, the reasons that I gave for the attraction of north Leeds were pretty much the reasons why this area was moving at a faster rate than the others as far as I could tell. However, although north Leeds was indeed showing signs of capital appreciation, it was not so noticeable that the average person in the street would have spotted it over and above the general rate in which Leeds was rising. A person such as me, actively looking for such minutiae, had to delve deep into cyberspace and all the information that is contained therein to have found it. And now that I found it I had to act... my 48 hours was up.

10

Found It

Still by this time I had not approached an estate agent. I had no need to. Driving around the area, coupled with my investigations online, had meant that there was no need for me to approach anyone on the ground just yet. I started to drive around areas that I had short-listed to see if anything took my fancy. This was the tricky bit. As you might imagine, there are a lot of roads in Leeds. Even though my search had narrowed the area down to north Leeds there was still a lot of driving, but really there was nothing else for it. This is the bit that you mustn't cut corners on. So fill up your tank with petrol (but don't if it's a diesel) and buy an A to Z.

Gut feelings

Earlier I mentioned that I get a gut feeling about a place; I do believe that we are all prone to those feelings. I think I am at a point where I am capable of understanding their meaning and what they refer to when it comes to something that I like (my wife says that she got that same feeling when she first met me – ooh she's such a liar).

After no more than two days of driving down preselected roads, I spotted a cracker. I turned down a road and liked the look of what I saw. It was tree lined, and high up on a hill. The houses were all grand Victorian terraces three floors high and very pretty. After nearly ten years of one-bedroom flats in the rough, tough areas that I had been buying in, I wanted something as far removed from that as I could get. This was pretty much it. At the better end of the road (I say 'better' as it was further away from the main road and hence the noise) was a house for sale. I knew it was a house as opposed to flats as it only had one doorbell.

Investigating

I took a look at the 'For Sale' board and rang the agent there and then, but did not tell him that I was actually there. I didn't want him to know that I was so keen. He told me that it was a 5-bedroom house over three floors and was on the market for £150,000. I asked the agent the only question that a person needs to ask and that is why the vendors are selling. He told me quite matter of factly that they wanted to move to Australia. 'Don't we all?', I said as the November rain continued to beat on my car's bonnet. I asked him to send me some details in the post and hung up. I was keen.

Viewing the property

Once I received the details I was able to see the interior and the layout. I had resigned myself to the fact that for this sort of money it was not going to be Italian marble and jacuzzis but it looked clean enough. So I called the agent back and booked a viewing. He did not turn up and so it was the vendor showing me round. On entering the front door I decided to buy it. I walked in to a wonderful wide entrance with a front door that was more than a metre wide. There was stained glass in the door with different coloured sunlight pouring in through it. The house faces east and thus gets the morning sun. It will, by default, get the evening sun in the back garden.

I noticed that there was little furniture around and the owner seemed to be alone in the house. There were photos of a child and a woman and he was wearing a wedding ring. It was a little peculiar, so I asked him why he was selling: Was it too big for him? **Vendor's Mistake number one:** He told me what the agent had also told me about his moving away, but that he was married with a little boy. I tried to push him for a bit more information and discovered that he was a teacher and had already got a job at a university in Australia. **Vendor's Mistake Number two:** I asked where his wife and child were, and he told me that they had already moved there and were renting until this house sold.

Making an offer

I now had enough information about the vendor to ensure that I was in a much stronger position should I want to put in an offer, and I knew that I would. I had my funds in place and I was chain free, and it went without saying that Mr Australia could not entertain an offer – no matter how great – if the potential buyer was stuck in a chain. He could sit around waiting in his lonely front room while his wife was paying rent for a house 20 billion miles away, but was that sensible? Either way, my first offer was knocked back. I am not going to tell you what it was; you'll laugh. My second offer came soon after: I wanted to show him that I was serious, so on advice I went in at £10,000 under the asking price subject to survey. He was reluctant but accepted.

Surveys

A survey comes in many guises, but when you are considering buying a property that is over 100 years old, it is imperative that you get a full structural survey. This will cost about £1,000 and it won't cost you anything. Why not? Well, when carrying out a full structural survey the surveyor will look at everything in some detail, especially on a house that is of this age. And to be honest, the surveyor is bound to find something wrong, unless it is absolutely turnkey – and this house was not.

You will always be able to approach the vendor with a better than reasonable chance of getting something knocked off the asking price due to whatever the surveyor has found. In all circumstances any offer put forward for property acquisition is subject to survey.

Negotiations

This surveyor decided that it needed a new roof at a price of about £5,000, and very soon rewiring. I went back to the vendor and explained that I couldn't possibly pay all this money now that I had to spend £5,000 on the roof. (The roof was the original roof and was starting to look tired, so my statement was not without foundation.) Via the agent, the vendor asked to see the report. I told him that that would not be a problem, but that the report had cost me £1,000 and if the vendor wished to see it then it would cost him £500 or he could get his own survey done at the price that I paid. After some to-ing and fro-ing, we met halfway and the price went down another £2,500.

Roofing

The roofer was working on the principle that anything that has been rained and snowed on for 100 years needs replacing, not that it actually did. In the end, as I always knew, I did not need a new roof and to this day have spent only £50 once when I initially bought the house. Victorian properties usually tend to have slate roofs, and slate is strong, although brittle, waterproof, light and readily available. It is unlikely that any of these factors will change with age. Slate does not become porous over time, it remains light and usually the only thing one needs to do to is to readjust the slates if they have moved or indeed replace the odd one, again using slate.

Many homes that initially had slate roofs have had them replaced with new roof coverings. These usually take the form of concrete tiles which are much, much heavier than slate. As a consequence, over time the roof starts to bow. This is clearly visible from the ground. This is because over time Welsh slate has become expensive so people have used cheaper alternatives, the consequences of which would not be visible until years later when possibly new owners are occupying the property. Now, Spanish slate is cheap enough to do the same job as before so there is no excuse.

Rental options

I went again to my trusted bank, the same one that I had used for ten years and still the same bank manager. I told him of my plan about buying property in Leeds and that I thought that it was a rising market. I gave him some comparisons with other northern towns and didn't even bother referring to London as it wasn't really applicable. I had also done some investigation vis-à-vis letting the property out, and was able to give him some numbers to help the repayment figures stack up.

Because this was a large five-bedroom house split over three floors, with a lower ground floor that could easily be converted if needs be, it would be very easy to split into flats or indeed rented on a per room basis. I did not want this option: five bedrooms, five individual people, one kitchen and one bathroom. Furthermore, five people with five different lots of friends means that there could have been as many as 15 people in the house at any one time.

The reason that I was looking at a new area was to realise some capital appreciation, not for the rent. Of course I would not just let the house sit there empty when it could be earning an income, but five lots of tenants meant that the house would be classed as a house in multiple occupation and as such would need extra works carried out to it in order to comply with current legislation. Moreover, when it came to time to sell, I would have to turn it back into a house in order to put it back on the market. So you see it was better for me to let it out as a house, as a single dwelling, and bite the bullet when it came to the rent.

Fortunately nearby was a lettings agent whose board I had seen on many properties in good areas. So I approached them. For the first time in my life I was approaching a lettings agent to get my property let. As my house was pretty much up to speed, the only service that I wanted from this agent was tenant finder. I have to say that even if my property had been in Timbuktu I would only have got an agent for tenant finder. The extra 15 per cent that they would charge for 'looking after' it, really is money for old rope.

If the property that you are letting out is a distance away from where you live, firstly make absolutely sure that the place does not have anything that is likely to need attention. Accidents will happen of course, but if you have an old boiler for example, that accident is going to happen even quicker. Set up a standing order with the tenant and arrange to go round on a regular basis but not too often; you don't want to become a hassle.

There is really no need to be giving away 15 per cent of everything you earn just to be on the safe side. When getting your house up to speed initially, you will get to know tradesmen in the area. If the tenant rings with a gas problem, send the plumber direct. No matter what he charges it is bound to be cheaper than the same price plus the agent's 15 per cent! But under no circumstances should you give the telephone number of tradesmen to your tenant and suggest that they call them direct bypassing you. You do not want to become lax, and you will get a bill for works that are now impossible to check.

Finding Tenants

I asked the agent for only families, and wanted a sizeable deposit reflecting the quality of the house.

After that, for four years of property letting using the same agent, I always got doctors. There is an enormous teaching hospital in Leeds called St James (Jimmy's as it is sometimes known). Doctors would come to the area and want to rent for six months to a year while they were searching to buy a house. So I had unwittingly tapped into this not exactly lucrative, but definitely regular, market. I will admit that this was luck not skill.

A good investment

The house is now worth £500,000 – that bit was skill and not luck. Earlier I mentioned how important it was to be patient when looking around areas choosing where you might invest. The road immediately parallel to mine has exactly the same type of properties, five-bedroom Victorian houses – these change hands not for £500,000 but £325,000. That is how important a difference one road can make.

11

London (she'll make you or she'll break you)

The Leeds house sale was completed in November 1999. The rent I was getting was £750 per month. I was hoping for £800, but signed a one-year tenancy and so cut the tenant some slack. The letting agent had done a great job finding the sort of tenant that I wanted in the house. It was a joy to have a tenant with a nice car and a decent job. A tenant that wasn't likely to re-divert benefit forms or steal my boiler.

Rising value

Coming up to Christmas things were going very well. Christmas came and went and the spring of 2000 brought about a real surge in the property market. It may have been the new millennium, it may have been everyone's computer still working one minute after midnight on New Year's Day, but whatever it was the market started to move upwards. This was the position that I had been hankering after – making money twice on the same deal. Each month I was being paid £750 by a tenant living in a house that I owned, which was also rising in value.

At this point it was difficult to ascertain exactly by how much it was rising. I would need more similarly-styled properties in my area to be put on the market. But other properties, the value of which I knew before Christmas, were now not only selling faster but also selling for more money. Three bedroom semis before Christmas were on the market at about £65,000; this type of property was now being sold at an asking price of £80,000.

It is as if there was a change in people's attitude in what they would and should do with their money. How much of it should they devote to where they lived? They started to realise that their home would not only act as a shelter to them and their families, but also rise in value. This would allow them to borrow more money because of the lift properties have seen. In the past if there was not enough equity in a property, lenders looking to put a second charge on the residence would probably not lend at all.

Borrowing money

Borrowing money secured on your house always carries a risk. The amount of equity in your home is roughly the amount that your lender will lend you, but it is still reliant on you earning enough to meet the extra demands carried by this second mortgage.

> If you borrow money for a new car that money is dead, as all cars depreciate in value. If you borrow the money for a structural addition to your house, your property will immediately rise in value. In turn your new larger house will rise by a greater amount than if it had remained at its original size, thus helping to refill the equity pot that you have recently just emptied. If you are desperate for a new car, do some work on your house first then go on a track day to get it out of your system; you'll get the best of both worlds!

I was able to see that Leeds was indeed rising in value. I had decided to buy one larger and more expensive property rather than go for two or three and spread my risk. There are times when either one can be the right thing to do and in this case I believe that I did the right thing. The area that I went for was definitely one of the better parts of Leeds, and the property that I went for would make, and indeed does make, a wonderful family home.

The ceilings are ten-feet tall and all the rooms are an impressive size. Compared to a modern build people would be struck by the difference almost immediately and would rather go for my house than another, even if that does mean losing something like parking facilities.

Interest rates

After some months as now a property speculator, as well as a property landlord, I felt comfortable that I had added another string to my bow. I had assumed, rightly or wrongly, that if interest rates started to rise it may indeed devalue my newly bought Leeds property, or more likely slow down its growth rate. But on the plus side, those interest rate rises might curb people's appetite for property acquisition in the first place and so push them into the rental market – people who may not have ever considered renting. I also had two types of property to rent now, a lovely large five-bed town house for an affluent family in a nice suburb of north Leeds, and the other end of the spectrum, one-bed flats for those that were caught, unable to escape even onto the first rung of the property ladder.

I did not believe for one second though that interest rates were indeed going to rise; quite the opposite in fact. Getting ever so slightly political again, the Labour Party had been very canny when they had entered office by remembering what had happened in the boom and bust times of the Tories some years earlier. Interest rates were at a level that inspired confidence in the market. I am not going to go any more into that particular episode, but people realised then that they had committed themselves to mortgages they could not sustain because of the incredible rise in interest rates. They had been implemented by the then government in order to try, at least, to keep a lid on inflation. It was of course the government that was responsible for any changes in interest rates.

New Labour were new to office, and they hadn't even had a whiff of office for 18 years. They didn't want to be caught out by making basic mistakes, especially as the country was indeed coming out of recession, so they handed all responsibility to the Bank of England. This ensured that it was the chef that was put in charge of the kitchen, so to speak, not the owner of the restaurant, and it further meant that there was a very handy scapegoat waiting to take the blame for any problems to do with all things financial.

However, there is a clause that stipulates that in times of crisis, the government of the day (so far it is still Labour) can take back full responsibility and all decision-making powers without the need for Commons' intervention. To date I am still not sure if they have indeed needed to take back control.

Rising property prices

So I felt fairly confident that property prices were going to go up. There was also another reason why I felt so confident: when I approached the bank for financial help, I knew that they would do their own investigations into what I had proposed. Thus, if they had come back to me asking for a large deposit, that to me would have signified that they had little faith in the market or were at least less bullish than me.

The fact that they were happy to lend without any extra commitment on my part filled me with confidence about how the banks also saw the market going. It was essential that although we were indeed singing from the same hymn sheet, the repayments were not more than the rent that was achievable. I had not worked out the repayments based on a rental of £800 per month – that would not have been bullish but foolhardy, and I do not think that the bank would have considered it sensible. I actually used a figure of £400 per month; I very much erred on the side of caution.

Asking the lenders

> Banks have an extraordinary array of skills at your disposal. As potential customers we should not be frightened to take advantage of this.

In this situation it made sense to me to ask their advice. Without actually communicating it verbally, their actions spoke volumes to me. Years later, I would need the services of the bank again although this time the sum involved would run into the millions. Once again I needed not only the bank's money but also their verdict on my plan, which was to purchase a sizable commercial enterprise. It was fraught with complications and even my own solicitor wanted out. My other problem was that all lending institutions wanted a deposit of 20 per cent and I was simply not able to find this amount. So I used a broker to find a lender that would lend on this project with only a 10 per cent deposit from me. We found one, and the fact that they were happy to lend such a sizable amount with only one tenth as back up from me, told me that it was a safer bet than even I had given it credit for.

Moving further afield

While the market was moving nicely upwards in the north of England, the market down south was slowing down. London by 2000 and 2001 had apparently reached its peak. And people had started to consider the north for good yields. The property that I had purchased in Leeds demonstrated to me that it was indeed quite possible, easy, in fact, to live somewhere and buy somewhere else.

I had been lucky in that I had found a lettings agent that was not only extremely savvy about the local market but had been there some years and so was able to give me accurate information about how things were, how they used to be and his thoughts on where they were going. They say that you can't look forward until you have looked into the past.

Leeds is also somewhere that I was familiar with, as I had visited it on numerous occasions, but it must be noted that the area that I chose to buy in was completely alien to me. The only part of Leeds that I understood at all was the city centre and as I mentioned earlier I had no desire to buy there. So as it turns out, Leeds might just as well have been Manchester as far as I was concerned. I took all this on board and started to consider buying more property in the North because of the slowdown in London then I had a Damascene revelation... in a mate's flat in Tooting.

This was a friend I used to be in a band with years ago. (He played bass and I played guitar – I'm still pretty handy today.) Anyhow, the first property that he and his girlfriend bought was a one-bedroom flat in Tooting Broadway. He was from Tooting Bec and really wanted to stay near his parents if he could, but in 2001 Tooting Bec, allegedly, was the new Clapham (probably because Wandsworth was the new Battersea and Fulham was the new Putney). Consequently Tooting Bec was totally out of his price bracket.

He started to look elsewhere, still trying to stay near a tube and the Northern line. He discovered that properties near St George's teaching hospital in Tooting Broadway were nearly half the price of those in nearby Tooting Bec. After a couple of weeks of looking, he put in a successful offer on a rather large one-bedroom flat very close to Tooting Broadway tube station.

Valuation differences

I used to visit Brian and Mikela a couple of times a year just to say 'hi'. On one such occasion Brian informed me that he had just had the flat valued by an agent (more out of curiosity than anything else). How much? £150,000. My ears nearly fell off when I heard that. Tooting Broadway, for the uninitiated, is nothing like Tooting

Bec, and it has to be said that it is rarely a person's first choice area to live. All you have to do is go there and see for yourself. I have to say that the agent's valuation for my friend's flat really caught me by surprise. I couldn't believe that a one-bedroom flat in a part of London that people have to live, rather than want to, was valued the same as a five-bedroom house in my leafy suburb in north Leeds.

Armed with this information, I considered two things:

1 Leeds still has a way to go and I was right to buy there. Maybe I should continue to.
2 All I had to do was to find other properties in parts of London akin to Tooting Broadway with good transport links, on the market at £100,000 or less, and the potential was there to earn £50,000 per property.

The second seems really too easy for some boffins to imagine, but I am a simple soul. Why complicate the equation unnecessarily? The hunt was on.

Investigating London

I already had a fairly general understanding of the geography of London and knew that there was indeed little point in looking for one- and two-bedroom flats for £100,000 in Chelsea or Knightsbridge. Indeed I could also discount Clapham, Battersea, Tooting, Wandsworth, Putney, Fulham... the list where I *couldn't* buy was enormous. So I changed my system, and began to look at areas where I knew I could buy for this sort of money, but where the properties would appreciate over time. I started to look at Croydon, Thornton Heath, Norwood and Crystal Palace. All these areas were affordable. The important questions were:

◆ would they rise in value?
◆ would they let easily?
◆ would they be easy to manage from 230 miles away?

Into Surrey

Croydon has a population of more than one million people (Leeds and Sheffield put together) and is actually in Surrey, but is about as far removed from Kew or Guildford as you could imagine. Croydon worried me because of its population; it feels dense. Crime figures for Croydon make it appear more like Compton in LA than Surrey. I didn't need any property that I bought in this area to be another statistic, thank you very much. Because of the population of Croydon, I was finding that the only properties within my price range were ex-council properties, or buildings that had once been office blocks now crudely converted into living accommodation. Both appalling.

Converted office blocks

I once went to visit such a flat, a penthouse no less. Two years earlier it had probably clattered to the sound of accountants working for some company or other. It faced south, was on the top floor, and had no air conditioning. It was boiling hot, and outside was not even really hot. All the windows were of the old steel variety that local authorities loved so much because they lasted forever. The floor was laminated and was already starting to lift, the kitchen was off the living room, the bathroom – although nicely done – was tiny and the bedroom was in another part of the building.

This had been purpose built as an office block, not living accommodation, and so the layout of the apartments were higgledy piggledy. This did not offer modern living for the modern person of today, where the living space flows neatly and seamslessly from one zone to another. In this case, the apartments had to utilise communal areas to get to other sectors of the same flat. Next door had also decided it would be a good idea to put a *trampoline* on their balcony for their little boy. Ah, bless. I wonder if he is still alive today 30 floors up.

Croydon was letting me down in all areas. Transport links were pretty good, but because of the population of the area it was prone to overcrowding. I couldn't see a reason why anyone would want to live there if they could live somewhere else and commute. So I started looking at areas that were within easy reach, but less populated and offering better value for money. Property that was more in keeping with what I had in mind. I had to remember that whatever it was that I bought, one day I would have to sell it on, so I wanted to make that part of the equation nice and easy.

> People will rent something that they may not necessarily love, but rent it nevertheless because it affords them everything that they need for the short term. Those same people however will be far more difficult to please when the time comes for them to buy their own property and part with tens of thousands of their hard-earned pounds.

Norwood

So I decided to look in the Norwood part of London.

I noticed that it was broken up into two sections: west and south. The west looked very nice, near to some lovely lakes and green areas, but transport let it down. South Norwood on the other hand was just the ticket. Closer to Croydon for shopping and work, and local shopping as well in the form of Thornton Heath. Not a million miles from Streatham (or St Reatham if you are a Two Ronnies fan).

I decided to take a closer look at the area before actually ringing any agents about specific properties that were on the market. I had another mate, who now lives in Canada, called Jason. He lived in Balham and came along with me to look around this area as he was thinking about moving. He and I were looking for different types of property but in the same area. I jumped at the chance to have him with me as I was already forming a plan in my head.

Striking lucky

As we walked along Holmesdale Road, near Crystal Palace football ground, I spotted a painter and decorator cleaning his brushes outside a small Victorian terraced house. He didn't look like the owner and so I asked him if the owner was going to move in or what his plans were. The painter said that it was his understanding that the flat would be going on the market. I asked permission to look round, and got it. The flat was the ground floor of the terraced house. Two bedrooms of an OK size, and newly refurbished. Brand-new kitchen and bathroom, full central heating, car parking at the front and a nice-size garden at the rear that was not shared with the flat above. Wow – this was just what I was looking for. The car parking and the back garden meant that it was very sellable afterwards as well.

The decorator had no idea about the price; why would he? I gave him my mobile phone and asked him to call the owner of the flat. He did so and passed the phone to me; the flat was going to go onto the market at £97,500. I got him down to £91,750 (using the excuse that he wouldn't need to give 2 per cent to an agent), and bought it there and then on the phone. He would fit carpets as well (not jumbo cord). One down, two to go.

Did I forget to mention I was on the hunt for three properties? I was more certain of the London market than I was of Leeds, especially after the Tooting Broadway episode. What I had to be wary of was the speed at which other people would discover this neck of the woods and force prices skyward before I had had time to buy. Afterwards that's fine just not before.

South Norwood seemed to me an area where people could live away from the mass populous of Croydon, yet it still had a neighbourly feel to it. In the mornings it had a wonderful train that started out life deep in the heart of Surrey but arrived at Norwood Junction station and then went on to Charing Cross without stopping.... home to the city in ten minutes was not something that even people in Kensington could easily boast.

Moving quickly

The manner in which I had bought the flat might have seemed a little gung ho to some, but it was an opportunity that I didn't want to pass me by. Had I waited for the flat to come onto the market officially I could not have used the agent's 2 per cent fee to my advantage. That 2 per cent fee on nearly £100,000 meant I saved nearly £2,000 straight away. I was also able to look around the flat without an agent breathing down my neck, and spouting all of their usual BS about stuff that I didn't need to know or already knew. Not because I was a clever dick but I had really done my research, and this was my business. I took time looking around, as there was 230 miles between me and it, so I had to make doubly sure that I was happy with it. The fact that I had a friend also helped as it enabled me to get a second opinion from someone that was not in competition with me (he was really after a house as he was married and already had a little one).

There were lots of questions that needed answering, not necessarily before I committed myself to the purchase, but at some point. Things like how the flats were split, who had what parking space, how much the service charge was and so on. For anyone buying a flat it is important to discuss the lease and in particular how long is left to run. In this case it was over 70 years. I had assumed that the freeholder of the house had probably split it into flats 25 or so years ago, lived in one and rented out the other, and then decided to leave altogether, selling them with 99-year leases on the pair of them. As it turns out, my vendor had only had the downstairs flat for a couple of years and had paid about £55,000. He probably spent £15,000 doing it up and was therefore set to make over £20,000.

As soon as I knew I was buying that flat, I went to the centre of Thornton Heath to try and find a reputable lettings agent. I wanted the same arrangement as in Leeds – tenant finder only. This would have been more of a gamble because of the distance involved between the north where I lived and London, but my principles still applied. Whilst I was looking I continued to search for other properties, and found a gem.

The search continues

I was always wary of properties that made bold claims about their size or quality, especially after the debacle in Croydon – the penthouse that was nothing more than a series of offices with a bathroom stuck on the end. But here I saw a penthouse that was the top floor of a block that had been purpose built as residential accommodation. Again it was in South Norwood, very close to the shopping parade in Thornton Heath. This was on the market over my budget, at £125,000, but looked to me to be a lot more accommodation. So I went to the agency.

> If you are in a good position when it comes to buying don't be afraid to show it.

I was looking for a further two flats and so when I went to the agents about this particular penthouse, I also told them that I was in the market for another. They consequently took me very seriously and gave me all the attention that I wanted. We went to the penthouse, and as soon as I walked in I was bowled over. It was a beauty. A massive 1,200 square feet. Two bedrooms, two bathrooms, 22-foot kitchen diner, 21-foot living room and of course, top floor. It came with parking. There really wasn't a downside. Yes it needed a coat of paint, but I loved it. There was a little crack in the bathroom that was slightly disconcerting and I made a point of exaggerating it to the agent. This crack had the potential to be something structural. I asked the agent my usual favourite question: 'Why does the owner want to sell?' He replied that he was moving away; nothing more ominous than that. I thanked the agent, and went home to think about the flat.

Negotiating

I was definitely going to put in an offer but the crack worried me and it was over budget. I made an offer at £110,000. No chance. The agent told me that while I was in a good position, the flat was worth every penny of £120,000 and that is what they had advised their client to take nothing less. I couldn't believe it – a decent estate agent. So I tried my old trick. I offered asking price, on the condition that the flat was taken off the market immediately. Then I would get a full structural survey done. All that was agreed and the flat came off the market.

My surveyor went round, just to value the flat, but I had asked him to give me his thought on the crack in the bathroom. A fortnight later he came back to me to say that the flat was tickety boo; the crack had probably been formed by the raising and lowering of the roof once in an extremely bad wind. Although this sounded like the end of the world he told me not to worry about it.

Using the survey

As soon as I had read the report, I rang the estate agent with a real sense of alarm in my voice. I explained that the surveyor was happy with the flat providing that the crack in the bathroom be taken care of, or at the very least, a sum of money be deducted from the asking price to allow the new owner to take care of it. The problem with the crack was that it was structural, and the amount of money we were talking about was £5,000.

The agent was shocked, and asked if he or his client could see the report. As was habit by now, I told them that it would cost them

£1,000, as that is what the report had cost me (in fact it had cost me £250). There was the usually to-ing and fro-ing and after a while things were not really progressing. Their problem was that they knew that a full structural survey would have cost about £1,000, and so my claim was definitely believable. But they had no way of knowing if I was telling the truth or not.

I didn't want this flat to slip away and knew they were getting frustrated, so I called the agent and asked for his confidence. I told him that while I would not show them the report, because I didn't think it fair that I pay for something that others get the benefit of, I would tell him about the roof. I knew full well that he would get a second opinion from another surveyor, even just on the phone. I was hoping that the other surveyor would confirm that for the roof to be lifted in a strong wind and then dropped back down was feasible.

Getting the upper hand

I then played the waiting game again. I say again, as I had noticed that it always took the agent a while to get even trivial answers back from his client. I rang and asked a young woman in the office if I could speak to someone about this flat. I also asked her why it took so long to get answers back about the property. Quite naively she told me that it was two friends that had bought the flat and that one had moved to New York with his job; they always had to wait to call him and get answers back. This bit of news was a revelation. It told me that one of them, at least, was impatient. He was paying for a mortgage and renting a flat in New York. They obviously wanted this flat sold, quickly.

The agent called back to say that he would meet me halfway and knock £2,500 off the asking price. Prior to speaking to that young woman in the office I would have taken that, but now I knew to be bold. I stood my ground and suggested that whoever bought the flat might well have to spend £5,000 repairing it. Why should I only ask for half the money? Furthermore, because this was starting to drag on, if I didn't get a decision by 5pm on Friday (lunchtime in New York), then the deal was off. In this case my bullishness paid off. They came back to me with the full £5,000 off the asking price, and the deal was done. Before you all start to throw rotten vegetables at me for being sly, the only porky pie I told was that the survey cost £1,000 as opposed to £250. I had told them the truth about the crack in the bathroom being the result of the wind lifting off the roof in a strong gale. I had simply got lucky by discovering the situation about one half of the selling team, and I was bold enough to stick to my guns.

> When you are negotiating, use your common sense and try to glean as much information as you can about whatever it is that you are trying to buy. Then use this information, always being aware that once you have set the precedent as to the direction in which you are going you cannot then turn around and be caught out.

Taking a risk

There will be an element of risk, as I knew when I made claims on my survey. Had the owner carried out his own survey he would have known that I was at the very least exaggerating the problem with the crack. The information that I got regarding the two friends splitting up definitely helped me understand their time-scale, especially where overseas is concerned. I used this by demonstrating my frustration at the time they were taking; I was prepared to walk away from the sale. The vendors could not have afforded to take that risk, as earlier I had demanded that the property be taken off the market once I had offered the asking price. This ensured that if the deal went belly up, they would have to start marketing the flat again from scratch. Let's face it: no one wants to do that.

By now, I had already let out my first flat by the Crystal Palace ground. I had asked the estate agent that was dealing with the penthouse sale if they could recommend anyone, and they put me onto a small agency in Thornton Heath. To my dismay the flat did not let straightaway, but took about four months. To be fair it was around Christmas time, so people were thinking more about egg-nog than rent repayments. Once the flat was let, things went very well. I was very happy with the couple that they had put in, and to this day I have never even met them; that goes to show that I have not had the need to go down. Even though I was happy with this firm of lettings agents, and although the new penthouse was a stone's throw away from them, I did not want to use them for my new acquisition.

Going upmarket

I fell into the trap of getting delusions of grandeur. I knew that two-bedroom flats let in Thornton Heath for about £750 per month, £800 if you were lucky, but I wanted more. I thought that the flat deserved more. This wasn't just a two-bedroom flat, this was 1,200 square foot, en-suite bathrooms, top floor, and no one running above you; TV and hi-fi noises were the preserve of those lower down.

Furthermore, the ten-minute train to Charing Cross meant that I could attract those that wanted to live in Battersea or Clapham Common, but who would have needed £1,500 a month for the privilege. So I tried to capture that market using the incentive that this was £1,200 per month, and bigger. I therefore approached agents that were more in tune with renters who could afford this type of property, and went to Battersea and Clapham to find them.

To be fair all the agents that saw the flat loved it, as I did, but they knew that although it was indeed a wonderful, spacious place to live, the area was not in the least bit desirable. And people who aspired to living in Clapham and Battersea would not particularly relish living in South Norwood. Bloody snobs. I was putting my case forward to the agents as best I could: the ten-minute train into the city, the local shops and so on. The agencies told me, 'Yes, Paul, that's all very well, but you don't have to convince us. We have to convince the clients, which will not be easy.' As it turns out, out of the three agencies that put the flat on their books, not one was able to secure even a viewing.

Coming back to earth

I bit the bullet, and went to my friend's in Thornton Heath. They suggested a rent of £800 per month. Within only a matter of days the place was let. Two Nigerian security guards who worked nights nearby took the flat on a one-year lease but would have happily stayed there for the rest of their lives it seemed.

I wasted about six months with the other agents and can only really blame myself. I would have been foolish not to at least try to get more rent for the flat. I knew the only way that this was achievable was by approaching those that were not from the area, as I did not think locals could afford the flat. After all, it was the size of a three-bedroom house, and yet I was asking a third again in rent. Nothing ventured, nothing gained. The market simply couldn't stand the rent I was asking. I was probably ten years too early for that sort of rent.

As I mentioned I had told this agency, and others, that I was on the hunt for yet another property, hopefully a two-bedroom flat again. I managed to find another very close to the other two. This was again a top floor flat, this time in a large converted Victorian detached house. The flat was of an OK size, nothing fantastic but fine. It too was newly refurbished, meaning that I would be able to put it straight up for rent without having to do any work to it. There was a major problem though. It had slipped; subsided. The owner said that it had been professionally underpinned, and he had the guarantees to prove it.

Underpinning

Underpinning is a massively expensive and labour intensive job, but necessary if your property has foundation problems.

It basically involves digging a hole of four feet in length by about two feet in width and at least two feet in depth by the side of the building. Concrete is then poured into the hole and left to set. Then four feet of foundation is left untouched and another hole is dug to the same specifications four feet further down. This continues all the way around the building in order to strengthen the foundations.

The owner of the property was foreign; I think Algerian. His English was fine and he was able to answer most of my basic questions, guaranteeing his solicitor could answer anything more detailed. The price was £97,500; about the right money. Obviously it had cost him considerably to do the underpinning but he was able to spread that cost over three separate flats. Of the three flats that were contained in that one building, only one was for sale. The other two were being let out and he was absolutely not going to sell them. It was as if he just wanted to release £97,500 for himself and earn a living from the rent the other two flats brought in.

Making the right offer

Anyway, be that as it may, I decided to make an offer. I had known that I would be going over budget with the penthouse and wanted to get as near to £93,000 as I could. But he wasn't budging. He wanted £97,500 and that was it. Furthermore, I couldn't play my usual trick by getting a survey done as he had one done after the underpinning and the whole building was absolutely fine. So I just coughed up, and put in the offer that he wanted. To be honest, this price was a little dear in comparison with the first flat I had bought. But the market had already moved on in those few months, so I was conscious that anything I was going to look at would have seemed poor value for money compared with what I had already bought.

I went to my solicitor and made him aware of this new property that I had made an offer on, and told him to expect a call or written confirmation from the other side. My solicitor had been dealing with all my property purchases for over ten years and he knew how I operated. I also trusted him; after all if you can't trust your brief, then you're in trouble. Worse still, if you can't trust your brief when you're in trouble, then you're really in trouble.

Getting help

Now you will recall that my friend (not the one that played bass, the other one), Jason, was also looking for a property in the area. He and I had made an agreement that if I were to find anything that I thought would be suitable for him, I would let him know as soon as I could – helping him to get a jump on the market. This was plausible for me, as property was my business and so I spent most of my day looking at property. Furthermore, because I was buying three properties, agents would approach me with places that were not even on their books to see if I was interested, and it was this sort of help that I was able to give Jason.

In return when I saw properties on the Internet that were within my price bracket I would ring Jason to drive down to the road and give me his opinion as to whether he would rent or buy a property there. He would let me know how far it was from the station, if there was a noisy pub nearby – that sort of thing. The system between us worked very well, and indeed this last flat had first been viewed by Jason, before me. He called and suggested that I take a look. He had also been made aware of the subsidence problem and had notified me of it.

When you are considering buying a property that is some way from where you actually live, be as efficient as possible.

Jason was in a position to view properties and their areas on my behalf. He did this for free as I was helping him, but even if I had paid his petrol, it would still have been much cheaper than me driving down each time to view them. Furthermore, because he and I had been friends for many years he knew what I was after and could speak to me candidly. He also had nothing to gain from my buying in these areas so his judgement was completely impartial.

Going nowhere

The two previous property purchases had gone smoothly enough but this third was taking its time just to get going.

After three weeks, we had still not heard anything from the other side. I spoke to the estate agents who had themselves tried to contact the owner, but he was abroad. Finally a solicitor's letter arrived. It was really very standard and didn't mention anything about the sale, just that someone new was dealing with it. Weeks lapsed again; by this stage I was getting frustrated by the whole thing. Our letters were not being answered and the deal was not progressing. The flat was sitting empty while I could have been earning £750 per month.

I was also starting to worry about the deal in general. This market was rising quickly and if the deal fell through I did not want to feel as though I needed to rush into buying another. Months had now lapsed and our letters were being answered at a snail's pace. Information that we required about the underpinnings guarantee was not forthcoming; details about the lease, nothing. We finally managed to ascertain that the other side's solicitor could not speak a word of English. My solicitor finally got him on the phone and the only words that he was able to say were, 'Yes,' and 'Thank you'. As a joke I told my solicitor to ask him to get permission to sleep with his wife, and see what answer he got.

Learning from experience

After six months of getting nowhere I called the agents and told them that if we hadn't exchanged by that Friday, I would pull out. Guess what: we didn't. So I pulled out. Six months of my life wasted on that fiasco. And my fear about the market moving on was very well founded. Two beds were now out of my price bracket, especially because I had gone over budget on the penthouse. Ex-local authority properties could be had for a song, but they were ugly and I knew they would be difficult to let and even harder to sell.

I am not sure if there is a moral to this tale of woe. One just naturally assumes that the other side's solicitors are at the very least going to have a basic understanding of not only the language but also the Law. Strangely, after I pulled out, I heard nothing from the owner of the flat via my solicitor. If my solicitor had cost me the sale of a flat I would try to resurrect the situation and probably get another solicitor. It was as if the owner didn't want to sell the flat and so gave the job of dealing with its sale to an incompetent buffoon.

12

Running London

I was very angry and bitter about what had transpired with that third flat. It was not only lost potential income, but it stopped me from continuing my assault on the south east London property market. I had come to London with a plan, and due to something that was completely out of my hands was unable to carry it out.

There were some positives to be drawn from it though:

- The market had indeed moved on, meaning that my two other properties had risen in value.

- My standing with the bank was as strong as ever, and my predictions were all successful. I would be able to approach them with ever more ambitious projects knowing that so far I had a 100 per cent record, apart for my second-hand car venture of course.

I could have remortgaged the other two flats to help raise the finance needed to buy a third, but the amount by which those two had lifted was still, by this stage, not enough to guarantee suffi-cient funds for the safe acquisition of a third property. Furthermore, banks would have seen it as slightly risky. They would still have probably lent the money but I would have had to stump up more in terms of a deposit. I was still working on the premise that these properties would eventually sell for around

£150,000 or possibly a little less, so I did not wish to be too bolshy and get ahead of myself.

Taking stock again

But I had to pull myself together. Things do not always go to plan in business and, as Meatloaf would say, 'two out of three ain't bad'. It was now time to take stock again of where I was. It wasn't too long ago that I had last taken a look at where I was, but I had spent more on just two flats in London than I had on my entire portfolio in the north of England. Borrowing £25,000 is very different to borrowing £300,000. So, if for no other reason, I wanted to keep a check on my nerves.

Both of my properties were let in London, my house in Leeds was let and all my North Lincolnshire property was let. It is very unusual for anyone to have all their properties let at the same time, especially if they have more than a dozen places. There is usually something empty, but just for this brief period I was able to put the 'No Vacancies' notice out. Of course it didn't last, it never does. But this was how I ran things for about 18 months, trying to keep things tight.

The properties in London were running as regularly as clockwork, and this was my main concern. They were so far away that any problems meant four hours down the M1 for me and then four hours back again, as well as having to contend with the labour charges as supplied by tradesmen in the great smoke. It is never easy for a northerner to comprehend just how much builders charge in London when they know full well that the prices do not reflect the work involved.

Whatever you buy, you just have to swallow it or do your best to make sure that you limit the possibility of something going wrong. I did just that with the two flats that I bought. The first was newly refurbished and nothing was going to go wrong with it for years to come. The penthouse was quite new, having been built in the early Nineties, and after my coat of paint it was ready to go.

Keeping on top of the maintenance

In London I had really geared myself up to purchasing the right sort of property at the right sort of price. I had done my research into the areas and had assumed what the market would be in five to seven years time. Because of the distance between where I lived and London I had to make sure that both properties would not require any urgent attention. This was not strictly true of Leeds however. I was slightly more casual about Leeds and spent more time looking at areas than actual properties.

You will remember that I knew I was going to buy the house as soon as I walked into it, and that is exactly what happened. It was over 100 years old; the flats in London were either more modern or had been redone. Because I was more eager about the house in Leeds, as it was my first foray outside my hometown, I really wanted to get it let as soon as was practical. This meant that I cut the odd corner. The boiler was as old as the hills and French. Really hot water never came from that system; it was just enough to stop you from freezing. The radiators, as a consequence, got fairly warm but again you couldn't cook on them.

Anyway, my 'it will be all right' attitude came back to haunt me about a year after the house was first let. For that entire time, I had been getting requests from the tenants about changing the boiler. Changing a boiler for a five-bedroom house would have cost me about two months rent, and I really didn't feel that the boiler needed replacing as it still worked at about 65 per cent throttle (I've known cars work at less than that).

Spoiling a break

I kept putting them off, until one weekend when I took my family to Euro Disney. Upside down, on a roller coaster, my phone rang. I answered it, and actually put the phone to my bottom thinking that it was my head (remember I am upside down)! We righted ourselves and the phone ended up by my ear (how much more confusing would that have been in Australia?!). It was the tenant from Leeds.

I knew he was going to grumble about the boiler, so to start with I pretended to be the French operator and spoke in a monotone voice giving him suggestions in French. All I wanted to do was fob him off for three days until I got back to England, but he was cut off. I then tried to call him, but to no avail. For the next two days he and I played phone tag; neither one of us managed to get the other. The long weekend at Euro Disney, for me at least, turned into a wait-by-the-phone exercise. Finally he got me and I was back in England the next day to sort out the boiler once and for all.

I could have avoided all this by simply getting organised at the beginning and getting that boiler taken care of when I bought the house. Now, although I was no worse off financially, I had a tenant that was less than happy with his landlord. For the first time I knew I had made a mistake, and felt guilty that I had not acted properly to start with. We live and learn.

Heating systems

The London properties were in fine fettle though, nothing to worry about there. The penthouse flat had storage heaters throughout. There is really nothing to go wrong – they are a series of heat-retaining bricks wrapped in a wire. The wire gets hot by electricity that has been taken by the system after midnight when the electricity is cheaper. It is then stored in the heaters until you decide how the heat should be distributed throughout the next day, either all in one go or spread out at a lower temp for the next twelve hours. Two thousand years ago the Romans used bricks to heat buildings. So much time has passed and we still use this system, as well as pumping hot water around pipes in order to heat our homes. Not really very sophisticated!

The flat also had an immersion heater. These are small tanks of water that have a large element that gets hot and heats the tank. The water in the tank is static and so takes a while to heat up. When it is gone you must wait a while before using it again. It works rather like a large kettle. The system is fine, and immersion heaters very rarely go wrong. If they do they usually need another element (£20 and £30 to fit: you could almost do it yourself). The other flat had a combination boiler, but that was brand new and came with a two-year guarantee, so I knew that I had trouble free lettings for that time.

On returning to England I went to the house in Leeds to see about this boiler. I had always been told that old boilers, before the intervention of circuit boards, were relatively simple beasts and that it was usually pumps that went wrong on them. The problem with this boiler was that it was very old and very French, meaning that parts were not readily available and they were very expensive. In the end a new boiler was required and that was that.

Changing a boiler

When changing a boiler, if you replace it like for like and keep it in the same place, the job will be simple and thus inexpensive. Remember that plumbers like an easy life; re-routing pipes all over the house is time-consuming and expensive and not a job they relish.

To be honest, I would have greatly preferred for the boiler to have been removed and put somewhere else, but the only place for it was one floor up. The plumber got out of this job by quoting a massive amount, and in so doing got me to keep it where it was.

Investing again

After I had taken care of the boiler job, I realised just how well things were going in London. I had virtually no problem from either tenant. One of them was even starting to make noises about buying the flat that he was in, he was so happy there. It flattered me but was not in my game plan. The market had still not risen sufficiently to make this worthwhile – I had only owned the flat for 18 months or so and a return of ten or 15 thousand pounds was not enough.

The lettings agent had done a great job in finding tenants for both properties. They were not only let, but on no occasion did I not receive my rent and I had no reason to believe that the properties were not being looked after. So I began considering investing in London again, staying in the same area. Now that the dust had settled after the debacle with the solicitor who didn't speak English, I was on the lookout again. This time I knew of a foolproof system that guaranteed the rent would be paid and that the properties would be left in A1 condition.

The Council

At that time, in certain parts of south London, local authorities encouraged owner occupiers to consider renting out portions of their properties to help alleviate some of the council waiting lists. I got wind of a system that was being operated by Croydon Borough Council, whereby a private landlord could let his property to the council for an agreed sum for anywhere between one and five years. Your rent would be guaranteed and the property would be returned back to the landlord in the condition that it was given to them. This was too good to be true. The council would effectively be the tenant.

I made some further enquiries, and discovered that it was not actually the council that ran the system, but a body that was backed by the council, working in conjunction with the council… that was good enough for me. I approached the relevant department who passed me onto another, who then passed me onto another, until I finally spoke to someone who knew what I was talking about. The system was indeed as I had been led to believe, with a few clauses:

1 Although it was possible to sign a lease for up to five years, there would always be a break clause for either party to take advantage of after year one. This alarmed me, as if I got into bed with the council on this project, and they were able to bail out after only 12 months, it didn't instil confidence in the deal as a whole. Nor could I approach a lender guaranteeing five years of relative safety.

2 The standard to which the properties had to be handed over to this council-backed enterprise was astonishingly high. They required the standard of the property to be over and above the standard of those rented out by the private sector and those rented out by the council themselves.

3 The owner of the property was responsible for the cost of the buildings insurance on the entire building, not just the proportion that was his responsibility. On a house split into two flats I would have to insure the whole house, then bill the upstairs separately. As well as this, it was also incumbent upon the owner to take out three-star gas cover for the duration of the let (at this time it was £15 per month – £180 per year).

In addition to all this, you would not receive market rent, but about 10 to 15 per cent less.

After I had digested all of this, it didn't look like the fantastic opportunity that it had seemed just a few months earlier. As is usual with me, when I had learned of this brilliant money-making scheme I was hoping to go into it on a grandiose scale. Not by letting a single flat to the council, but rather by approaching them with the notion that I would buy an entire building devoted to this system of letting. Now things were decidedly different. The owner would have not only ongoing bills – the insurance and gas cover – but have to suffer a hit in the rent, and negotiate the tricky business of the one-year break clause.

I still approached them with my plan, hoping that they would be able to work out another system for financial partners (me). No dice. In fact they were against the idea of my buying property for them, as it meant that they would be obliged to use these properties and any changes to their system of operation would hit them harder because of their involvement with this new venture. That is why there was a break clause after one year, it allowed them to jump ship if required (the removal of the first-year break clause was something that I had suggested, for obvious reasons).

Number crunching

In the end I did not pursue it. It was a lot of hard work for very little reward. When you do the numbers, it could end up costing money:

- ◆ Rent for a two-bedroom flat in SE London: £750 per month.
  Minus £112.50 (15 per cent)
  Equals £637.50
- ◆ Three-star gas cover for one year: £180
- ◆ Buildings insurance for that portion which is yours: £300
- ◆ Doing up the property to the standard the council demands is anybody's guess, but let us say £1,500.

The first year's bills, therefore, come to £1,980. The first year's earnings come in at £5,670. If you do not go with the council you would still have to insure the building at the same price so £750 × 12 = £9,000 minus the £300 insurance.

You can see that it would take nearly two years to earn the same amount using the council-backed organisation as if you were to stay as a private landlord in the private sector. You would also not be able to review the rent after a period of time, so your flexibility as owner of the building is removed.

I could, of course, have continued to look at London. With hindsight it would have been lovely to have invested in central London, but prices at the time made me feel uneasy and central London was not seeing record growth levels (unlike today). It also worried me that with the amount of property available in central London, another added to the list might just sit there forever and a day, looking to get let but not actually getting let. So I got the jitters about central London. The outer areas were getting too dear for me, and the rents were not really covering the mortgage with enough to spare to make me sleep comfortably at night.

An interest-only mortgage being lent on £120,000 at 5 per cent would mean a repayment of £500 per month. Over two years a rent of £750 per month (£18,000) and a mortgage repayment of £500 per month (£12,000) is a difference of £6,000. That's fine, but if your tenant signs for one year, and leaves, it can take you four months to find another (that is how long it took me with a specialist in the area). Then the figures look decidedly different: rent accrued £15,000, mortgage repayments £12,000. This does not take into account wear and tear on the property, insurance costs, repairs, agent's finders fees and so on... so it really becomes essential that the property realises some capital appreciation in order for this miniscule amount to become worthwhile.

13

Realising Some Capital

We are now in 2003. I had owned my property in Leeds for four years and my properties in London for two years. I decided to get everything that I owned valued, including all my properties in North Lincolnshire.

The one-bedroom flats that I owned in Scunthorpe had not risen by so much as one penny. I knew that they wouldn't which is why I decided to buy in Leeds – here I had a result. After four years the Leeds' property was now worth £275,000: double what I had paid. The London flats had also risen in price. The first flat that I bought near the football ground was now valued at £137,000 and my penthouse £187,500. This was really much better than I had anticipated. The plan had been to try and realise £50,000 in five years with both flats, but I was able to realise over £70,000 on just one and around £35,000 on the other. Between them I had my hundred not in five years, but two.

Making decisions

This was indeed good news. Not only were the properties that I had bought worth a lot more than I had anticipated, but I had been earning rent from them all this time. I was in a good position and started to think about the future: how to convert that equity into cash. What would I do with it? Should I just stay put and see how things play out for another year? There was a lot to think about and I didn't want to rush into making a decision.

A hiccup

Then one morning at five o'clock my phone rang. My two Nigerian tenants had called at this ungodly hour to tell me that they had accidentally singed a corner of one of my kitchen cupboards. I knew that no one would ring me at 5 am to tell me something so trivial. I told them to stay put, as I would be down straight-away. Four hours down the M1, and I arrived at the flat... they had burned down my kitchen. I was speechless. My wonderful 21-foot kitchen was black. As bad luck would have it, the units had burned and the oven hood caught fire – it was this that caused all the black smoke, everywhere.

They started to tell me a story about putting on a pan, but I didn't believe them. After nearly two years in the flat they had never done anything this idiotic. Furthermore they had rung me at 5 am, and they work nights – they could not have started the fire. I decided to wander around the flat, and I opened the door to the living room only to discover a young lady sleeping on a mattress. Aha! The cause of the fire. I kicked the mattress to wake her and proba-bly shouted 'Oi!'. Sleeping Beauty didn't bother to pretend that she was asleep. 'Did you make that bloody mess in my kitchen?' She would have been pretty silly to admit it. The two tenants contin-ued to take responsibility for it, which I had to admire, but either way she was not allowed to be there. Apparently she was a cousin from America; cousin or not, she had to go.

I went back into the kitchen and didn't really know what to do. There was black soot everywhere. I was insured but the tenants couldn't live there while the flat was in that state, so they moved out. I was disappointed; I had got to know them and for nearly two years everything had been fine. Now my wonderful £187,500 penthouse apartment was ruined.

Fixing things up

To be honest though, it looked worse than it was. I came down two weeks later to take the keys from the tenants and decided to stay a couple of nights to try and see how much it was all going to cost. The kitchen was actually OK, it was just the hood that had caught fire and made the mess. Fortunately all the doors in the flat were fire doors, and had been shut when it happened, so the soot did not dissipate throughout the flat and ruin all the carpets in the other rooms. The mess was pretty much contained in the kitchen diner. Still, it all needed sorting out.

I pretended to my wife that I was going to take her down to London for a show and a slap-up meal. Once there I set her to work scrubbing the walls while I shampooed the carpets. Of course it was a blatant lie but my wife realised when she married a landlord that she married into the job – a bit like a policeman's wife. Yes she complained, especially when I used to stop for cigarette breaks and kept telling her that she needed to wash out her water more often, but in the end we nearly got there. After a whole weekend of scrubbing and washing, the flat was a lot better but the walls and the carpets were not in a good enough condition, and I had to admit defeat. My wife did her best but it was not good enough. It looked like I would have to replace the carpets and redecorate.

Deciding to sell

Sometimes something will happen that seems a tragedy, but out of the flames of the fire rises a phoenix. Had the fire not happened, I would have been quite happy to keep collecting rent from that flat for the rest of my life, but maybe this was the kick in the backside that I needed. I considered that the valuation that I got for the flat was probably as much as it was ever going to realise, so I decided to sell up. In its present state there was no chance, and nor did I want to take a £30,000 hit for £5,000-worth of damage.

I went ahead and fitted a new kitchen. I definitely paid more than I should have, but I couldn't go to the flat day in day out checking on workmen on different stages of the job – there was 250 miles to consider. I approached one firm that would take out the old kitchen and appliances, dispose of them, fit a new one, re-plumb it, re-routing any pipe work necessary, and make good any damage that they did. This probably cost me an extra £1,500, and I was happy to pay that for all the headache that it saved me. When finished, the job was first rate and I was very happy. Once that was done, I spent a long weekend painting the flat myself (if it's not wallpapering I can do it), and once that was done I had the relevant carpets refitted.

Finally, it was time for it to go on the market. I had never sold a property before. After 13 years of buying I didn't know what to look for in an estate agent, so I thought of the obvious. I wanted a firm that knew not just the area but also surrounding areas. An agent that might have several offices all around the south of London so different offices could pass information to each other. If I could glean any information about them, vis-à-vis the way they conducted themselves in business, then all the better. In the end I went with Townends. They had offices in Thornton Heath, Croydon and all over the south of London. I considered this to be ideal – I thought about the very real possibility of people going to offices in Tooting or Balham and being priced out of that area, but whose details could then be forwarded onto the Thornton Heath office. I would be able to snap them up, a veritable alligator waiting in the rushes for my penthouse-wanting victims. It turned out to be November by the time my flat was ready to be put on the market. The agents had suggested that we try before Christmas just to get a feel of the market. I thought it was a plan and so gave it a go.

On the market

November and December were very slow. Dead in fact. January was also dead – not one single viewing. The agents suggested dropping the price. It is amazing that virtually all agents resort to dropping the price as a first approach rather than a last. Agents, remember, work on commission, so you would think that they would be eager to keep the price high. In their eyes, 2 per cent of a house *not* selling isn't worth a damn, but 2 per cent of the same house, less £20,000, is at least some money in the bank. Of course this is true, but it also means to hell with the vendor.

I was not prepared to drop the price purely to make things easy for my agent. If my property was on the market at an inflated price then I would understand, but that was not the case. The price would stay: £217,000. I know it is more than the valuation, but don't forget my new kitchen, and two tins of Dulux paint as well as some very expensive net curtains that I put up in the kitchen; you can see it all mounts up. Moreover, as we were putting it on the market before Christmas just to test the waters, I thought that we might as well be bullish with the price just in case some wide boy from Wandsworth fancied a penthouse flat to show off to all his friends.

February came and went and still nothing. Reluctantly, acting on advice, I dropped the price to under £200,000. March, April and May came and went and I was getting worried. The agents claimed that they were showing people round but that the flat was still too dear. I didn't believe them. In my mind, if someone is genuinely interested in a property, views it, but considers it too dear, they at least make an offer in the region where they feel comfortable. It may not get accepted, but unless they offer, they will never know. As you all know by now, I have never had much luck making cheeky offers, but at least I have given it a go. (To be honest, I never had much luck asking out beautiful women, but I still did it. One day I got lucky, and now several years later we are married with two children.)

Changing agents

I finally got fed up with the agents, and decided to jump ship. I went to a much smaller agency right across the road, who suggested putting it on at £187,500. This was of course my bogey number. It was the valuation given to me almost one year earlier but he insisted that it was the correct sort of figure. There had never been a flat of any description put on the market in South Norwood or Thornton Heath at that figure before so we were in unchartered waters. It was a Friday and I gave him the OK. He told me that he had a viewing the next morning with a young lady and that it felt promising. Very promising in fact because she offered the asking price. £187,500 – within three months the flat had sold. I repaid the bank what I owed and pocketed a very swift £70,000 (I don't mind sharing that with you as I have nothing to hide from the tax man). A few quid in my pocket at last.

Meanwhile I was still collecting rent from the ground floor flat that was near Crystal Palace. The tenant was still making noises about buying the flat, and this time I was taking the whole matter more seriously. The only problem was that he didn't have the money. He was able to go to £100,000, but that was the valuation from two years ago and the actual price was nearer £140,000. Unfortunately he was unable to find that amount and I think that he was concerned he was renting when he could have been buying, so because we could not resolve this matter he put his notice in. I understood, but didn't really mind as I could now put it on the market.

I went with my new smaller agent and it went on the market at £137,000. It sat there for three months without a viewing. Although it had two bedrooms, one bedroom was off another and so it wasn't a proper two bed, but nor should it have been priced as a one bed, so we sort of split the difference. In the end it sold for near £130,000. I was still very happy, as after I had repaid the bank I was in profit to the tune of £100,000 over both flats. Make no mistake, if I had had this amount of money ten years earlier, I would have been getting about in something low, fast and Italian. But with a wife and two children, one of whom was a baby, I had my duties as a father and breadwinner to consider.

A change of direction

I realised that this money was as a direct result of my properties appreciating in value and that the rent was merely covering the loan repayments and a bit on top. I was starting to get a little fed up with the whole job of being a landlord, and preferred instead to become a property speculator: a person who takes risks on the property market just by hoping that it will rise in value and then sells it on in order to release the equity to finance something else. I started to look at what I considered to be markets that were ripe for investment – I started to look abroad.

14

Overseas Property

Owning overseas property is always the ideal. Every time I saw *A Place in the Sun* I have to admit I used to get ever so slightly jealous. Buying a property abroad is not too difficult. What is difficult is making that property work for you and earning a living from it.

Now firstly we have to consider what 'abroad' is. In 2003, the euro had been in place for three years and had stabilised at around €1.40 to the sterling pound. The American dollar was also weak against sterling, it being around $1.91 to the pound (being at war with just about everyone can have that effect). I wanted to look at places that were not in the public consciousness yet; there was nothing clever about following everybody else. Besides, I had done quite well out of investing in a part of London that others had either avoided or not thought to look. The same could really have been said of Leeds. So I was happy to go where no man had gone before. Indeed, looking at these places ensured that *if* they turned out to be hot spots then getting in so very early would mean that providing I was not in a hurry to take my money out, I could be set for some very good returns.

Where to start? I have mentioned that the American dollar was sitting at its lowest level for 15 years and so to not take advantage of this would have been silly. But trying to buy in American dollars does not necessarily mean buying in America. The Caribbean, the

Bahamas, South America as well as Mexico all trade in dollars. I started by looking in America: Florida.

Florida

I know that Florida has for a while been an area that has seen many people invest in the rental markets offered by Kissimmee because of its proximity to the large theme parks. You were almost guaranteed rental income from these properties year round, and the properties didn't need to be anything special: just clean, near the parks and with everything working. Florida is always warm – January until December, with the summer months being excruciatingly hot. But Florida has so much more to offer than just Disneyland. It has the Cape Canaveral space centre on the east coast, and the Daytona race track about 50 miles to the north. To the south is Miami and Key West. There are also huge swathes of marshland that are the habitat to countless birds and aquatic life, the most famous of these being the Everglades.

Orlando

I started to look into Florida but deliberately avoided the area around Orlando. I didn't want to get caught up with the masses of people who buy homes for themselves to holiday in twice a year and the rest of the time let the properties out. I was not convinced that there was that much money to be had by doing this, especially on a small scale. Local laws prohibit foreign house owners from letting their properties out all the time thus limiting the amount of revenue that can be achieved to start with.

Furthermore, agents charge a fortune to maintain properties, sometimes a fifth of the rent. Then there are pool cleaning bills, garden maintenance, income tax, repairs… the list goes on. Not only that but properties that are let to holidaymakers get more of a beating than those on long-term lets. Families with children on holiday are hardly going to worry too much about carpet stains and mess when they are in and out of the pool splashing water everywhere, and playing beach football in the living room. Once that family from hell have left the next ones are just about to move in, so don't forget to triple the amount in your column that reads 'cleaning'.

I had the advantage of being a seasoned campaigner when it came to property letting, I might have had to deal with my issues in colder weather but the problems were just the same. So I was not necessarily looking for a rental proposition, nor one where holidaymakers were going to be in and out every five minutes. I was trying to find a balance of an area that had the potential to rise in value and yet could accommodate holidaymakers who would be more inclined to stay for longer – maybe even the whole winter at a time. Orlando did not offer me this, and while the area to the south of Florida was indeed very beautiful it was not an area that would attract holidaymakers to stay for the long term. The Everglades, in my opinion, was a day trip, anyone staying for three months was a scientist. I did consider Miami, but again was put off by the size. I thought that it would take me too long to get to know it well enough to be able to buy there shrewdly. Because of its population, and links with the drug trade, I would have felt a little uncomfortable knocking on a door on a Friday night asking for rent from a Latino named Chavez with a cocktail stick in his mouth saying, 'You talkin' to me?' So it was no to Miami and to the south.

The West Coast

The east coast of Florida, however, seemed to have it all going on: Cape Canaveral, Daytona Beach, West Palm Springs, Fort Lauderdale (for spring break). It was close to the theme parks and in hindsight I have should have given this area more care and deliberation than I did, but I was sidetracked when I received a brochure on an area on the west coast of Florida – the Gulf Coast.

The Gulf Coast

Five or so years ago, developers were building homes on the Gulf Coast as if their lives depended on it, the area from New Port Richey right down to Naples. This area appealed to me.

I will admit that it had a lot less going on than on the east coast, but that is probably, in my subconscious, what drew me to it. I thought people would like to visit because it would be more peaceful than anywhere else. It would be more suited to older families whose children had grown out of playing beach football in the living room or having water fights in the kitchen. Moreover older people, maybe even retirees, might well be tempted into staying for the whole winter. Not just those from cold countries visiting but also Americans who had got fed up with their colder part of the USA. And if America is anything like Britain, the over fifties hold 80 per cent of their country's wealth, so affordability would not be an issue. I decided that this would be my area to concentrate on. Developers were moving in *en masse*, and if they had spotted something then I should have at least checked it out.

Finding the spot

I looked at areas such as Tampa, Sarasota, Venice, Naples (although Naples was very dear) and New Port Richey. At the time four-bedroom detached properties were going for about £150,000. These were standard houses with the pool included and a small back garden. Some of these properties were on canals and included boat docks, and some were inland in small, artificially created, villages with everything you would need on tap. I started to really look into this, and was happy to buy straight from a developer.

Americans are very keen on buying brand-new homes although here in the UK I do not think we are so bothered. Developers offered guarantees for build quality and were able to source the best land. Furthermore, the mini towns that were created meant that there were bound to be other people in a similar position to me. We could exchange stories and ideas, as well as possibly being able to help each other out with the property management side. I took all this very seriously. A whole year went by and I still hadn't decided what I was going to do. I just couldn't make up my mind. The amount of property that was on offer was staggering and in so many different areas. As soon as I had decided where I was going to buy, another website would appear offering more benefits, but this new development would be 100 miles north. It was like chasing a chicken; you think you have it cornered then you're off running again. Meanwhile I noticed that the market was rising. Properties that were on the market a year before for £150,000 were now being sold for £175,000. I didn't want to daydream forever but nor was I going to rush a decision. So I carried on looking, being steady and patient. I knew what I was looking for and I was sure that I had found it, several times, but it was as if there were many properties that seemed to fit the bill. While all this research was going on, I had also decided to explore another part of the world so I could hedge my bets: Europe.

The reason that I had decided to go after a purchase in dollars was because of the dollar's standing in relation to the pound. The euro also afforded this luxury and this is what initially caused me to look at countries within the Eurozone. But there were plenty of them, and not necessarily offering the potential property growth that I was after. So again I had to decide where I was going to look.

Italy

Being Italian, I dare say my aunty would hope it would be Italy. But at that point Italy hadn't won the World Cup since 1982, and as us Italians have high expectations of our football team I was still in a bad mood about that. As well as that, all my family are in Sicily and they would have considered it a snub to have not bought there.

Italy, although a very beautiful country, is also extremely diverse. A drive from Milan to Rome in October can require a raincoat and jumper at the start of the trip and Hawaiian shirt in 85 degrees at the finish. The same cannot be said of a drive, at the same time of year, from Leeds to London! Temperature and climate aside, Italy is a changing country, politically and economically. The beautiful villas in Tuscany and Umbria are expensive and can sit on the market for years rather than months.

There has been a tendency recently for the younger members of the towns and villages all over Italy to go to university and become qualified in something, anything; just as long as it means they can work and live in the larger cities: Milan, Rome, Turin, Naples. This means that these once bustling villages, that had charm and spirit, might retain the charm but have lost the spirit, along with the younger generation.

Young, modern people of today want the speed and style the larger cities offer. They want busy bars not sleepy cafés. They want the opportunity to earn a wage that will enable them to kit themselves out with all the material trappings of a modern world with a sexy apartment to house them all in. I suppose it is what the same generation wants all over the world; Italy is no different. Italy, once famous for food, sports cars, fashion and family is now only famous for food, fashion and sports cars. Family ties are no longer strong enough to hold communities together, and it is the small towns and villages that suffer.

So I was put off Italy. I would have had obvious advantages in buying there. I am able to speak the language for a start, and I have enough family to use any property that I bought there, ensuring that it wouldn't get damp and was occupied more often than not. Italy is also a country that loves its red tape and bureaucracy and dealing with several sets of officials just to repaint a house filled me with dread, not to mention earning any rent on a place or selling it on later. So really, quicker than I thought I would, I discounted Italy, probably because I was more familiar with it than if I had not been Italian.

France

I wanted to think more clearly about what it was that I was after from my European property. Was it the same as my American adventure? Apart from the difference in where it was. Then it became clear: surely the whole point of Europe was its proximity to the UK? Anything that I bought in American dollars was going to be at least seven hours away, but I didn't want to feel that I had to get on a plane just to cross 22 miles of English Channel. It became obvious that I should at the very least have a look at France.

France is a colossal country, and until recently I didn't know that it received more foreign tourists than any other country in the world: 60 million a year.

I think of France as being several countries in one. The wine-making region (I know all of it is wine-making, but I am thinking more about the south west). The south of France, the Cote d'Azur, where all the beautiful people live and escape their tax obligations. Northern France with its First World War battle scars, wonderful countryside and its closeness to England. Paris – Les Champs Elysées, La Tour Eiffel, La Place de la Concorde, Notre Dame, the Seine (with its newly installed sandy beach), the Palace of Versailles and so on... There is also the part of the Alps that affords skiing holidays; possibly not on the same scale as Austria or Switzerland, but nevertheless it still helps represent a country that has it all. All I had to do now was decide which bit I fancied having a look at.

Investigating the north

As it turns out I ended up looking at the north. You see, as well as investing in property, letting out properties and speculating in Leeds, London and now abroad, I had also decided to get a job. I was a property manager for a firm in Yorkshire, looking after 110 houses in Wakefield and in Huddersfield and some in Leeds. I simply do not have the time nor the inclination to tell you what happened there, but because it was extremely time-consuming. The only time I had available to view properties was at the weekend or bank holidays. So on one of the bank holidays in May I decided to go to France. I had to be able to go and come back and see the area that I was interested in within three days, so that meant it had to be the north.

I used my trusty Internet (by this time the Internet was broadband and all singing and dancing) and looked at the north of France. It was really still too early to pick out individual houses at this stage but I was able to arrange appointments with agents all over the area. I had discounted Pas de Calais as it was really too close to the ports and the tunnel. As such I thought that it had lost its identity and had just become a place where people stayed ready to board a boat or at least go somewhere else, a bit like the southern part of Kent. So the search started for me in earnest in Picardie and Normandy. But just before I left for the great unknown I decided to look, not at a road map as I had been doing, but at a general atlas of the area. I realised fairly promptly that the area that I was trying to cover and understand in detail within three days was about the size of Scotland. Still, undaunted I set off.

Arriving early

I booked a Eurotunnel crossing for Saturday morning and I left Leeds at 2 pm on the Friday before. It took forever to get down. The M1 on a Friday afternoon was somewhere I knew should have been avoided at all cost but because of my excitement at the trip I ploughed on, hoping for a break that didn't come. The Dartford Tunnel (actually the Queen Elizabeth Bridge going clockwise) was solid. Miles and miles of traffic; everyone desperate to get home. I just had to sit it out. Finally, I made it out and carried on down the M25, then onto the M20 all the way down. By this time it was getting late, about nine o'clock and I was definitely starting to get tired. I would be glad to have seen a hotel or B&B. My plan was to stay somewhere then to catch the tunnel in the morning. As I drew closer to the tunnel I started seeing signs, and before I knew it, I was at a gate ready to board.

'I'm sorry I think I've made a mistake somehow. My ticket isn't until tomorrow morning' I said to the boarding officer.

'Don't worry love, you can travel now for no extra charge. It's up to you,' she told me.

I thought about it: a hotel room in France or a hotel room in Folkestone. It's all the same really.

'I'll go now,' I said, and off I went.

The Eurotunnel is fantastic, especially if you get seasick like me. I was in France in a flash, but by the time I put my watch forward an hour it was past midnight and I was properly knackered. I am sure that my car realised how tired I was and just took me straight to an Ibis hotel. I had no idea how I got there, but I did. I coughed up at the reception and went to my room. It was very slick, with a sitting area as well. I didn't do too much channel-hopping as I wanted to get an early start, so pretty much straight to bed. Night, night.

Getting the lowdown

The next morning I woke at 6 am, as I had instructed my mobile, and I was downstairs at breakfast within 30 minutes. There was no one there apart from a young waiter who was obviously from North Africa. I guessed Algeria, given France's long-standing relationship with that country. I struck up a conversation with him, more about what I was doing there than he, and I have to say that I learned more from him about the area of France that I was trying to cover than a whole week on Google. There is simply no substitute for a person's experience. He told me exactly where to avoid and where to go. He suggested Hesdin was somewhere to avoid, as it was not very pretty.

On my drive down the coast I decided to drive through it, and have to say he was right. It had obviously had an industrial past, but all that was left were large rusting buildings and an aging population. I actually had an appointment with an agent in Hesdin; I rang him and cancelled. He was upset and asked why, so I told him straight. He said that there were nicer parts, but that would be akin to going out with a girl because she had nice legs but unfortunately a face like a melted Easter egg. I told him the whole place had to be nice, not just a bit of it.

Some of my waiter friend's suggestions, although quite accurate, were a little pricey. Well worth it I am sure, but just not what I was hoping to spend – places like Le Touquet on the coast. It is sometimes referred to as Paris by the sea, and has a Parisian price tag to boot. So I ended up driving still further south. It was not that important to me to find somewhere by the coast. If I had been looking in the south of France then that would have been a different story, but the northern part of France had such wonderful countryside you simply couldn't help but be hypnotised by it. I could easily buy a place in the country, surrounded by all the fields.

On the hunt

Somehow I ended up in a small town just inside the Normandy / Picardie boarder called Neufchatel en Bray. It was very pretty and I stumbled into an immobilier called Dubuc. Guillaume Dubuc spoke perfect English – too good in fact. When he asked me where I was from, I discovered that he had spent ten years of his adult life living and working in Leeds, so we were already sort-of related.

I asked to see what he had in the locality and also asked for some advice on where was best to buy, hoping he would tell the truth. He pulled out several properties that he had on his files and told me that the surrounding area was very pretty and made for a lovely vacation area. I had worked out that we were about one and a half hours by road from Calais and I didn't want to be too much further south. All the properties that he showed me seemed all right and so he asked Collette, who also spoke English, to take me round to see them.

Typical French style

I wasn't impressed. On arriving at number one, the first impression was good. It was a nice house set in beautiful gardens of about half an acre. The downside was that it was a little far away from anywhere so you would need a vehicle just to get a packet of smokes. Nevertheless, we ventured in. The ground floor was, I suppose, typically French. It was a good size, very rustic with a large inglenook fireplace. It also had a lovely large living area with the kitchen off it, which I thought was quite modern, and two further small reception rooms. So far so very good. The problem came upstairs.

The house was listed as three bedrooms, and from the size of the downstairs I assumed that the upstairs was going to be bordering on palatial in size. I was very wrong. The French have this awful habit of forgetting to create a corridor on the first floor of their houses, and so even though it did have three bedrooms, they were configured consecutively. This was made even more inconvenient as the only bathroom was downstairs. Just imagine the chaos when some old relative sleeping in bedroom three needs to go for a jimmy; they have to walk through bedrooms two and one, then back through bedrooms two and one to get back to bed. That person will definitely become *persona non grata* by morning, let alone by the end of the holidays. That was enough to completely put me off. To be honest the house was a little too far from civilisation to be considered a real contender. House number two was very small and house number three needed far too much work.

When considering a property to buy abroad, especially in a country where English is not the mother tongue, everything has to be a little easier than if it were based in the UK. Think about silly things that you would take for granted. Maybe at home you would have a car for all the adults, and everyone knows their way around. Abroad that would not be the case, and so while it might seem ideal to have a place in the middle of nowhere, the practicalities would mean that even the most trivial jobs need planning and forethought.

I got back to the office really unimpressed, and told Guillaume as much. He said he would go into the back room to see if anything had come onto the books recently. While he was gone, I took the liberty of having a look at the files that he had perused earlier, and I spotted a cracker. Lovely and big, it seemed nice and neat from the outside. I didn't know its location but I took the risk and put the file on his desk underneath some papers, just poking out enough that it could be spotted. On his return, carrying yet more tosh that had probably been sitting in his agency waiting for a roast beef like me to wander in, I 'spotted' the corner of this file on his desk.

'What's this?' I asked, in such a convincing manner I impressed myself.

Guillaume was confused, 'How the hell did that get there?' he must have thought. He pulled it out and I took a closer look. It was within my budget and looked fine. I asked him where it was and discovered it was only about a 20-minute drive from the office. This of course begged the question why he hadn't shown it to me. He fluffed his way through some answers, still confused as to how that file had ended up on his desk. I asked to see it and once again poor Collette was chauffeur.

Finding a gem

We arrived in the small town of Aumale, just inside the Normandy border. A very quaint little place with a square that had markets twice a week. The drive to the town was very scenic and I thought that this could well be the place for me. Once we pulled up I was very impressed. It was a large detached house with detached garage and separate office building. We got to the front door, which looked more like the entrance to a castle than a regular house. On entering we were greeted by the sight of the ceiling on the floor. They had suffered a burst pipe over the winter and consequently the water had poured onto the plaster ceiling. The damage was really pretty bad; it had affected the kitchen, hallway and living room.

Assessing the damage

Collette said that was why they hadn't shown it to me. But why didn't they just say that back at the office: 'Sorry, Paul, there is a problem with the ceiling and the house is a bit of a mess.' It really didn't quite add up. I wanted to look round the rest of the house, and found the source of the water problem upstairs. It was now repaired so it was just a question of putting right the damage.

The house, damage aside, was beautiful. Enormous. Downstairs there was a large living room, large kitchen, office and two bedrooms, one of which had its own en suite. There were French doors leading out onto a terrace that, because of the hillside location, was about 15 feet off the ground. The view from the terrace was breathtaking, looking over the whole valley and the countryside. It really epitomised what French views are all about. Upstairs the house had four proper bedrooms with another bathroom. The rear garden had a stream that contained trout and there was also a small orchard within its half acre of garden. All in all this was it.

The house was divine, the town very pretty and the house's location in relation to the town itself could not have been more perfect. It was rural, yet a walk into the main square would take five minutes, so really the best of both worlds. The only problem that I saw was the damage caused by the water. I did not mind looking at houses that needed redecorating, but really nothing more. All the stories I knew of French builders filled me with dread, but I did not want to lose this house because of my fear of French builders and allow someone else to walk right in and steal it. I kept quiet and asked Collette to take me back to the estate agents.

Taking a chance

Guillaume was at his desk having a coffee and asked me what I thought. I told him,

'I'm not surprised you didn't want to show me the house, Monsieur Dubuc. All that damage – I will be very surprised if you ever sell it. But to be honest I am a little stuck. I have to return to England tomorrow and really do not have any more time to look at more properties, but so far what I have seen has not impressed me.' I then went on to list all the shortcomings of the properties that I had seen – I was of course not being miserable – there was method in my madness. After that little rant I sat still quietly for some moments looking, and trying to feel, exasperated.

'I know I will look a fool, Guillaume. I will have been all this way from England, devoted myself to just one agent, and returned empty handed. I don't want that, so I am going to go for one of the houses that I saw. The big one with all the damage.'

'OK, he said. How much do you want to offer?'

I went in at a figure so low I actually risked being smacked in the face, which I would have taken with good grace. But believe it or not, Guillaume said that he would put that offer to the vendors and ring me in England. The offer that I made was based on the fact that I would have to put right all the damage internally, make good and redecorate.

He and I shook hands and I returned to my hotel in Abbeville. Next morning I was on the road back to Calais.

15

The Bahamas

Once back in England, I began to concentrate on the dollar again. There was no time to waste. I had taken a deviation from Florida for a little while, as it was starting to become confusing. Although I continued to look there, this time I looked at other areas also, still making sure that I was able to make the purchases and any subsequent purchases in American dollars. So it was back to the Internet.

Narrowing the search

I was able to narrow down my search by first ascertaining where I could buy in American dollars. I was starting to veer away from America simply because of its size. Florida still confused me so although I didn't discount it, I definitely put it on the back burner. South America didn't really float my boat either. There had recently been the coup in Argentina where people lost all their banked savings, and Brazil was still a place that to me only conjured up images of shanty towns and gang violence. There are a lot of beautiful countries in Central South America, but their political persuasion undermines their stability. As a result I did not consider them viable. These were emerging markets that really needed more time to emerge. I was not the type of speculator to get into an area too early, especially when the risks are that high. So I stayed in that hemisphere and looked at the Caribbean and the Bahamas.

These areas seemed to offer an investor many opportunities. They not only have plenty of sunshine, but they are known for it. They are also known for their easy, laid-back attitude to life and relatively low crime figures (Jamaica aside). They are also known, the world over, for those beautiful beaches and wonderful sunsets. There is also the advantage that they are as close as could be to the USA and Florida. One of the things that had put me off Florida was the size of the area and the amount of tourists there.

> The size of an area will have a bearing on the speed in which properties rise in value. If there is a lot of good buildable land, then there is the opportunity for developers to continue building in areas that have got too expensive. As a result those prices rise disproportionately slowly compared with other similar areas that are simply smaller in size.

A group of small islands only has a finite amount of area in which to build. Therefore, a bit like central London, the prices continue to go up. Once an island has been built up to its maximum there is nowhere else to explore.

I took this view on board and started to investigate these areas. I didn't bother to look at already known places like Barbados, Antigua or the Turks and Caicos. In my opinion these are already so well established that anywhere that was cheap, or represented good value, was obviously that way for a reason; I didn't want to be the sucker that thought it was a deal. So I looked a little off the beaten track.

I wanted to stay as close as I could to the United States as I assumed that this would be my primary source of business. Furthermore, direct flights from the UK still needed routing from Miami so the closer I was to Florida the easier it would be not only for Americans but also Europeans. After setting my parameters I had to concentrate on just the Bahamas, saying farewell to the

Caribbean as it was too far south (Barbados is around 1,500 miles from the nearest part of the USA whereas the nearest Bahamian island is 50 miles away).

The Bahamas are a group of islands numbering many hundreds, some of these not much more than raised levels of sand sporting vegetation. The islands that people know are Grand Bahama, New Providence capital Nassau and Paradise Island. All the other islands are now affectionately known as the Family Islands. I was not alone in looking at these places; I had started to receive literature from new developers wanting to explore what these Family Islands had to offer. Again I took the approach of not bothering with the already established areas, as I couldn't see the point.

> Being last to discover an area will not necessarily mean little yield, but it will mean less than if you got in earlier.

The Family Islands

It was important that where I chose to look had to be accessible by air as well as water. Imagine going to visit your home away from home, looking forward to your vacation for a year, and being stuck on an island for three days because the sea was too rough. So airports were a must. I also tried to find something that was unique to the island, something that could set it apart from others.

Remember that there were hundreds to choose from. I had to be careful not to just close my eyes and put a pin in the map hoping that that was the next property hot spot. I had to do more than just research the area. All these islands were beautiful, many had airports, more again had lovely beaches and were developed enough to cater for tourists without being too touristy. But there had to be something that just set it apart over and above the others.

Back to France

Then the phone rang, and it was Guillaume. My offer had been accepted – I couldn't believe it. The house I had wanted all along and would happily have paid more for, was going to be mine for a song. Please believe me when I tell you that I am not exaggerating this house. Six bedrooms, two bathrooms, half an acre of garden, its own stream and orchard. Sitting on top of a hill with unbroken views of all the surrounding areas yet a stone's throw from the town. The cellar, *le cave*, had ten-feet high vaulted ceilings and windows, as well as several doors to the outside. It would have made an enormous self-contained flat in itself.

Well, as you can imagine, I was chuffed. I had bought a house that opened up new possibilities. It was 90 minutes from Calais and thus the Eurotunnel, so it was not beyond the realms of possibility to commute to London – maybe not every day, but certainly twice or three times a week. France is one hour ahead of the U.K. and so once in England you can catch an hour back. Apparently there is a Eurostar train that leaves Lille in the morning and arrives in London only four minutes later (of course it isn't really four minutes later, but rather one hour and four minutes!).

As well as this proximity to the Eurotunnel, it is also 30 minutes south of Dieppe, 45 minutes east of Rouen (where Joan of Arc met her fate), and an hour and 15 minutes north of Paris. It really did have everything on tap. Guillaume and I proceeded to exchange details about money and addresses etc. and I had to hand over a 10 per cent deposit immediately. (This deposit is non-returnable unless the other side pulls out of the transaction.) Once this was done it was a question of sitting and waiting. Back to the Bahamas.

Getting back to the Bahamas

This little break in my Bahamian adventure enabled me to get back to my quest with real vigour, finding it all fresh and new. It also coincided with some more literature that I received from a developer looking for funding for a project in Abaco. There are actually two islands with this name, Great and Little (do you suppose that one is bigger than the other?). I looked into these islands and while they were indeed typically Bahamian there was nothing about them that really set them apart from anywhere else. It was while I was looking here, though, that I decided to look at an island that was about 30 miles south of Great Abaco, called Eleuthera.

Pink sand

This island is 110 miles long but only two miles wide. There are three airports on the island – one at the tip, one in the middle, and the last at the toe. Very convenient. There is also another island that sits very close to it called Harbour Island. This is so exclusive that it is only inhabited by Hollywood's glitterati, and can only be accessed by boat from Eleuthera. Eleuthera is very close to the US mainland and is accessible by air from Miami and Nassau, as well as a boat trip from any of the larger islands or Florida. One side faces the Atlantic while the other faces the calmer waters of the Caribbean sea.

Fishing here is world class, but to be honest much of the Bahamas boasts that; at least Eleuthera can boast it as well. Marlin, bone fish, tuna – all the usual that wealthy Americans pay handsomely to fish for, or go from Florida on their own boats to fish for themselves. But the *pièce de résistance*, this island's real Unique Selling Proposition (something, as it turns out, that nowhere else on earth can boast) is that the sand is pink. Don't get me wrong – it is not shocking pink, but quite subtle. Nevertheless it is still pink.

So I had found my island, with it's very own unique feature. It seemed to have it all: good airport links (all three of them), proximity to America, good fishing, beautiful beaches (pink ones), known by the beautiful people from Hollywood and relatively undiscovered by developers. Now I had to zero in on what I was after.

Exploring the area

Eleuthera also had another island within literally a few metres of its southern point called Windermere Island. It was a favourite with Princess Margaret in the Fifties, as well as other socialites from around the world. And it seemed strange that the great and the good knew about Harbour Island and Windermere Island, but not the big one in the middle. Maybe that was the problem. The fact that it was too big and thus these stars could not be assured privacy from the general public nor the paparazzi (I know how they feel). So I still felt confident about continuing my exploration of the area.

Property problems

One thing I discovered very quickly was that because the island was as yet unrealised by developers, the properties that were on offer were either vastly too expensive as they were built by wealthy Americans in the Fifties, or they were properties built by those indigenous to the island, usually of wood and poorly constructed. Thus anything that came on the market that was more realistically priced did not offer good value for money. Nor did I think that they looked like the sort of properties that would impress Europeans or Americans.

Doing the deal in France

Just as I started feeling frustrated, the phone rang again. It was Guillaume, letting me know that all the papers were ready for signing and that it was best that I go to France for the signing and the handing over of the keys. The date was set, and I took my wife on a long weekend (no scrubbing involved this time) to the town. We stayed in a hotel as the house had no beds or heating and it was a nice way to get to know the area a little better. The day came when we saw the notaire and all the forms were signed. I was told of one or two ancillary bills that I was responsible for, like the cleaning of my portion of the stream (£12 per year) and other local taxes, and that really was that. Apparently I am the only Englishman in the town, or I was then at any rate, so it really does go to show that in this case I had got in very early indeed to take advantage of this new hot spot.

The plan with this property had always been a long-term one. Rural France has never been a fast buck – a city centre flat in Paris is a million miles away from here. I knew that to begin with and had calculated my figures appropriately. I considered this to be a ten-year investment, something that would move along steadily. I was hoping it would rise by about 8 per cent per annum; I didn't consider this to be unreasonable.

Best of both worlds

Its location and proximity to beaches, and areas such as Euro Disney and Paris, mean that it would have an immediate fan base with the tourists. The fact that it was less than 90 minutes from Calais meant that commuting was also achievable, especially at a time when so many TV shows were talking about almost the entire population of England moving over to experience the good life France could offer. I erred on the side of caution here, and did not really believe the sort of figures that these TV shows were quoting. If I had, half my street would have left, so I wanted to stay as close as I dared to Calais without actually being there, to allow people who still worked in England the flexibility of com-muting. I always find it difficult to believe that intelligent, sane people will pack up their bags and head off to a foreign land and hope for the best. So I thought long and hard about this venture, but considered that this part of France really did offer the possi-bility of living and enjoying the French life while still commanding an English pay cheque.

At the time of writing, my six-bedroom house has doubled in value after just four years. I am sure that much of that has been because of the boom in the British housing market; affluent Londoners looking for a second home in the English countryside have been put off by the prices and the crime statistics so have turned their attention to going across the Channel.

A safe environment

To date, my house has been left wide open on two occasions (don't ask me how), and on both occasions the neighbour climbed in through the window, locked up, then left through the front door. When I order oil for the central heating, *le chauffage*, the cellar door is left wide open so the firm can refill the tank; they then lock up and leave. It is my total feeling of comfort and safety with regards to this area that enables me to leave the house unattended for long periods, knowing that all will be fine. Being a second home there isn't really a lot to steal, and squatting in rural France is a term that probably isn't even in their vocabulary.

I am, therefore, extremely contented about this purchase. It is not only rising in value at a faster rate than I had anticipated, but it is very usable as a holiday home and even a first residence for someone who does not need to commute every day to London or the South East. These will be the statements that I will use when it comes time to sell.... if that time ever comes, as I may just retire there.

Investigating the Bahamas

The deal concluded and the mini-break over it was back home to concentrate on Eleuthera. If I remember correctly I had started to become frustrated with this island. There didn't seem to be any property that fitted the bill nor my budget. Furthermore, it was not only relatively undiscovered by developers, but undiscovered full stop. Trying to find a map on the island was an impossibility. Yes, Grand Bahama and some of the more known islands, but not this one. Online was much the same story, even worse in fact. Aerial shots, the topography of the land, even basic photos or statistics of the larger towns, were not easily available. So with some speed, out of necessity, I became a super sleuth. I had to try and piece together information about the island as and when I learned it. Any opportunity to get a photo or picture of a section of the island went straight onto my wall. I started to get to know more about the area, and considered the possibility of buying land. I had never bought land before; I had thought about it being the prequel to building and it sounded like a lot of aggravation that I did not really need. But in this case there really was nothing else for it. I was pushed into looking at land.

Looking for land

On the main island were one or two small local estate agents that looked after the property that was for sale, and one or two large American ones, Coldwell Banker and Christies being the two biggest. I went onto their websites trying to get more information about the price of land and what I could afford. It became immediately apparent that the side of the island that faces the Atlantic is the side with the beautiful beaches. The other side, that is far quieter, is rocky. It would have been nice for this to have been the other way around, but I was in no position to alter it. Whilst I was looking, I came across some plots of land that formed an area known as Rainbow Bay.

Rainbow Bay

Rainbow Bay is an area in the centre of Eleuthera that was popular with Americans in the Sixties. They came here to escape city living at vacation time, and loved it so much that they have since come here to retire. There is a long-standing community of people that have known each other since the Sixties. They have joined together to form a group that now has the force to be able to carry out works to the locality without government intervention. Works to the infrastructure, such as re-tarmacking roads and rebuilding shelters destroyed by hurricanes and storms, were now the preserve of these industrious and obviously very proud new citizens. They came from an era where if you wanted something doing you had to do it yourself else you might be waiting for a long time. I liked the feel of the area, I liked the way everyone was extremely proud to be living there and wanted to maintain it as best they could.

So I tried to seek out land that was for sale. At first I went to the big two agents, and they had plenty on their books. Land that had come onto the market from sons and daughters left these parcels of land in wills from parents that maybe had a dream of retiring there, but whose children had no wish to do so. And there was also land being sold by those canny enough to have bought plenty of it 40 years earlier hoping that it would realise something eventually. Either way I was not exactly spoilt for choice, but I had a good selection of plots. Plots on sandy beaches cost the earth, as I expected, but plots near the coast, but on rocky beaches, didn't.

> There are three laws to be aware of when buying in the Bahamas:
>
> **1** If your property borders the beach, the public have a right of way across the sand but not into your garden.
>
> **2** Properties near the coast can only be built one-storey high, so everyone can see the sea.
>
> **3** If after you have bought your plot you wish to buy another, you are not allowed. This is to stop people buying too many plots and artificially dictating the market. You can buy another if you develop the first.

(I didn't actually know about the third one, and it did catch me by surprise.) I finally found a plot that fitted the bill. The price was within budget and it looked straight out to sea. It was in a small cove and thus was sheltered. It was about 15,000 square feet and could easily accommodate a three-bedroom villa with room for a pool and parking.

The cost of building

Building on any of the Family Islands is an expensive business. Everything has to be shipped in and the taxes on building materials are huge. This means that any property properly built to new hurricane standards by a reputable American builder will be expensive. Add to that the cost of the land which it sits on and you will realise why there is such a price gulf between properties.

I mentioned earlier about very expensive properties for sale; this island is still unchartered territory as far as even established agents in the area are concerned. In 2002 a property known as Helios House in the region known as Palmetto Point went on the market for $4m. One year later it was still there; two years later it was still there only with a price of $3.75m. Another year went by and the price was down to $3m. The house finally sold for $2.5m. Did that buyer get a good deal or was that the correct price to begin with? To answer that one has to consider other properties that are of a similar type, and their value.

Some agents will put a certain extra value on a sea view, for example, over a country view, or on the cost of fixtures and fittings – especially on an island where the cost of shipping-in these luxuries is truly staggering. When you also include taxes, then it is easy to see why some properties may, on the face of it, seem comparable but in reality require a different price. The difficulty is two-fold: firstly gauging the amount by which the price differential should be set, and secondly finding a buyer that will appreciate these differences and pay for that privilege.

It is my opinion that this island will in the future represent good value for money. Its size will enable enough people to come and enjoy what it has to offer, while not being so small that it will only be able to cater for the seriously well heeled, as with Harbour Island and Windermere. The fact that it is so narrow also means that no matter where you are, you are only one mile from the coast, and never more than a few minutes' drive to a sandy beach: yes, a pink one.

Eleuthera is large enough, and already populated with enough people, for it to be worth a gamble. But, as mentioned before, there are many islands that are nothing more than sandbanks and these can often come on the market. Be sure that whatever island you consider it actually has a rock base. Otherwise the parable of the man who built his house on sand might just apply to you.

Doing the deals

I used an American solicitor from Nassau to handle everything, and it turns out that the vendor was someone from New York. Everything went to plan and within one year that plot of land doubled in value. I had a feeling that something like that was going to happen, aided not just by the weak dollar, but also the relative strength of the euro. Rich Germans and English were also starting to buy anything in dollars. It was this that prompted the Bahamian government to introduce new laws trying to curb overbuying by rich foreigners looking to make gains in the property market.

So as I said, providing you start to build on your first plot of land, then you can buy a second. Fortunately I sneaked in just in time with my second and bought just before the laws changed. I had been invited to join the Rainbow Bay website and participate on the forum. This was a great opportunity to speak with those looking to sell their plots of land. I was lucky in finding someone that wanted a quick sale and was not so savvy with the market. I offered him the difference between what I paid for my first plot, and the new valuation. He agreed, and so I had my second – as luck would have it, 100 metres away from the first in the small cove. Now time has moved on and both plots have risen significantly.

I have not looked into building yet, as I know it will not only be expensive but also need my full attention, whereas plots of land can just sit there without any need for too much involvement. To this day I have still not even visited the Bahamas, such was the accuracy of the photographs that I was able to ascertain exactly what I was buying. Before the arrival of the Internet, a purchase such as this would have been an impossibility because of the time and costs involved.

The Internet has the ability to make everywhere seem just moments away, an e-mail is sent and replied to within minutes, but travelling to these sometimes far-flung places can require changes of aircraft, days journeying, different time zones and in the end you end up asking yourself if it is all really worthwhile.

Decide what it is that you are looking for in your property. Be flexible, like I was flexible in changing to acquire land as opposed to buildings in Eleuthera. Understand as best you can the area that you are searching and do not forget to consider the political climate. People are currently experiencing huge problems in Spain with the land-grab laws. Those affected lose their properties with no compensation whatsoever. This is a person's dream shattered by a law in a country in the EU not two hours' flight away; consider the possible ramifications of buying in countries on a different continent where English is not the first language.

16

Emerging Markets

What is an emerging market? I could tell you that Eleuthera is one. Now that people have started to buy there it is considered to be undervalued, underpriced. That is really all an emerging market is: somewhere that is undervalued (my wife always considers herself to be undervalued. Don't believe a word of it).

The significance of property

The word 'property' means different things to different people nowadays. To some, it means a place to live and be comfortable without any regard to what it will be worth in years to come. To others, the value of that property (and here I mean their own home) is so important that they will live in an area that may not totally suit them, but may give better returns in the long term. Because people are now in a position both to enjoy properties and earn money from them, they are starting to value their money-making potential ahead of their ability to enjoy them comfortably.

Without bragging, there was a period in 2004 when my house in Leeds was rising at the rate of £1,000 per week – that is not to be sniffed at. But it looks like the boom times here in Britain are all but over. With the rise in interest rates to 5.75 per cent, and the obvious slowdown that this will continue to have on the domestic market, it is little wonder that we look abroad to find some gains.

The Home Information Pack is now the law, and will curb property growth still further as well as making sure that those who want to move house, really want to move house.

Looking abroad for our property expectations to be realised financially is much more of a gamble than looking at home.

> I started out life by investing in my hometown. Then a town a little further away, then London. Then I made the decision to buy abroad. First France, then the Bahamas. France was close by and I could drive there if needs be. The Bahamas are a little further away, but they are an English-speaking nation. So I did it bit by bit, but all the time keeping strictly to my goal of what it was that I was after.

If I were asked where to put my money for future growth I probably wouldn't answer you as you might expect. You and I are different. I haven't even met you and yet I know that you are nothing like me. So how would I understand what it is that you are after from a property purchase? Really we have to look at it another way: we cannot ask what property can do for us but what property is going to do. Will that, in turn, suit us?

Working things out

I had an inkling that the city of Leeds was on its way up, and that if I bought in the right place I would be able to capitalise on the back of it. And I did. Remember – one road difference and I would be £100,000 lighter. I also considered that the area in which I eventually bought in London was undervalued.

I didn't need to read the Estates Gazette or sign up to property seminars about how to get rich. It simply took a conversation with my mate Brian, and the blue touchpaper was lit. I started my investigation on the area after I had realised that another area had got expensive (in this case Tooting). With both Leeds and London, my plan was to realise capital growth while still being able to rent the properties out to cover mortgage repayments.

My purchases in France and the Bahamas were purely speculative, looking for nothing more than capital gains. There was no prospect of being able to earn from plots of land in the Bahamas, and although the house in France could be let in holiday time, it required work and agents and cleaning and I was coming to the end regarding my relationship with tenants.

But generally there is much to consider when looking at areas that rise in value. We have to ask ourselves why it is that they should rise at all. What do they have that makes them such a worthwhile investment? And at what point should we go in?

Personally, I like to have a bit of proof that what I am looking at is indeed on the up. I will admit that Eleuthera was high risk and with no previous track record, but everything else had at least a hint that it was on the rise. Even my purchases in South Norwood had started to rise some time earlier, although I did not know it at the time. At the moment there are one or two places that are *de rigeur* 'emerging market' conversation topics at dinner.

Turkey

Ever since I went on holiday to Antalya, when I was 19 years old, I have liked Turkey. It has many factors that contribute to it being taken very seriously as an area for strong growth. The town of Bodrum rose by 25 per cent in 2006, outstripping central London and with better weather. Turkey has almost the same amount of coastline as Brazil. The coast that looks out onto the Aegean Sea has longer summers and milder winters than almost anywhere in the Mediterranean. People are sometimes a little nervous when they consider countries that are predominantly Muslim because of the problems with some fanatics who have caused terror around the world. It is difficult to dispel these fears, but I will say that Turkey is definitely a moderate country with very western aspirations. It does have a currency that changes like the wind; entry into the EU will help stabilise this and help Turkey's economic drive forward.

America and the Allied forces have needed Turkey's involvement in trying to settle disputes in the Middle East, Iraq and Afghanistan, as geographically it is a good base during these times of conflict.

It is also my opinion that Turkey may use this to their advantage when speaking to the EU once again about possible entry. This exclusive club now contains Malta, Romania and Bulgaria; Turkey's entry is a foregone conclusion. In fact, it is really only the French that are opposing their entry; there would be a massive influx of Turkish labour into the European mainland. This argument is not helped really considering that the new French prime minister is considering proposing a Mediterranean alliance for those countries that border the Mediterranean Sea – this would obviously also have to include Turkey.

Nevertheless, the French aside, properties on the coast in respect to Spain are still phenomenally cheap. Two years ago three-bedroom villas with seaviews and pools could be had for £63,000. That is no longer the case and those same villas will now be changing hands at around £93,000. It is my opinion that because of the price of these developer-built properties it makes sense, especially with one eye on the resale market, to buy the best you can. So rather than looking at two one-bedroom flats, go for a villa – detached if you can afford it.

> When considering buying abroad bear these thoughts in mind:
>
> If you buy two properties, one-bedroom flats for example, you will have to pay your agent two lots of fees when renting them out, two lots of cleaners will need paying, and two lots of bills as well as property taxes etc. A large detached villa bought in the right area will command more revenue than even two two-bedroom flats, especially if you have three bedrooms, air conditioning and a private pool.

The above definitely applies to properties in Turkey, and in particular on the Aegean Coast. It is also important to note that one of the criteria for Turkey's entry into the EU is that they have to resolve the North Cyprus dispute with Greece. If that means returning that part of Cyprus to Greece, you would definitely find another hot spot there. But it is a big *if*.

Yield: over 10 per cent per annum for at least five years... Easy.

Brazil

I was once on a TV show discussing overseas property, and another clever dick next to me said about Brazil, that if he was going to spend 12 hours on a plane, he would want to get off in the Caribbean. I understand what he means. Earlier I said that Brazil conjures up images of shanty towns and gang violence. I am being a little harsh here – there are other things it has going for it, but once you remove the carnival, and the Amazon, you are really clutching at straws. In order for a place to move forward one thing needs to be in place, and that is the ability to go to a football match and not get shot in the eye with a flare gun when trouble starts.

There are other factors too: political stability, economic stability, infrastructure in place, the ability to cater for tourists and their needs... the list goes on. I do not think that these things are as yet in place in Brazil.

It also has its size to contend with. Brazil is pretty much the same from head to toe; the same cannot be said of America which is also large but where one can find cowboys doing rodeo, the Statue of Liberty, Disneyland and climate variation more akin to different continents, not just different states.

Unless you have family ties in Brazil, I would not consider it. Other parts of the world are nearer, safer, more stable and offer more to the tourist and second-home owner.

Yield: over 10 per cent per annum over five years… No chance.

Dubai

Three years ago I saw an advert in the *Sunday Times* promoting apartments in Dubai, in particular studio flats for £33,000. Two weeks ago I saw an advert in the *Sunday Times* promoting apartments in Dubai, in particular studio flats for £33,000. Now if I had been someone that had bought a studio flat three years ago for £33,000, I think I would have the right to be pretty miffed at the fact that the same place could be had for the same money three years later. It's a different building, but let's face it, Dubai is Dubai and the specifications of these tower blocks are all pretty similar.

I also read an article in the *National Geographic* in 2007 that had great insight into the real cost of building Dubai and what is going on behind closed doors. It described in some detail the plight of the labourers that are being shipped in by the thousands from the Indian subcontinent to work like the slaves before them at a rate of $5 per day. This in itself is no wage to pay someone working in 120 degree heat, but when you also consider that they are hardly getting paid, then it comes into focus.

These labourers are living in shanty towns so awful that they would happily trade with those found in Sao Paolo. Open sewers run through people's bedrooms as they sleep on mud floors. All this was in the hope that when they left India they would be able to return with money in their pockets to provide for wives and children left behind. Meanwhile, Mohammed bin Rashid Al Maktoum apparently lives in the world's largest single residence, and has 60 people working for him within its walls catering for his every whim.

At night, gangs of Russians in less salubrious districts patrol the streets in cars armed with machine guns, claiming areas as their own while they look after their prostitutes that cater for the continuous influx of transient labour. The Red Sea floor has suffered irreparable damage because of the machinery used to create these idiotic man-made islands that satisfy people's need to be able to have absolutely everything they want, where they want it. In the old days, if you wanted a villa on an island first you had to find an island.

I do not consider Dubai to be a satisfactory place to invest, not just because of the shanty towns with the open sewers, or the gangs armed with machine guns, nor the prostitutes or the slave labour. The only things on offer are shopping malls, sunshine, and desert. You can get all that in Texas, with a rodeo thrown in as well.

Yield: over 10 per cent per annum over five years… I can't see it.

17

Over and Out

When people ask me what I do, I say I am in property. That is such a general answer, I might as well say that I am in the human race. As we know, property covers letting, developing, speculating, residential, commercial etc. etc. The move from one sector to another is not one that should be too daunting: a centre back asked to play on the wing is still playing football, and that is how you should regard property.

It is very difficult to write a list of dos and don'ts when considering going into the world of property. 'When you look at an area you should research it well' is so obvious a statement that it hardly needs mentioning, but it does also mean that you should not be blinkered in not considering other areas for potential gain simply because it may mean diverting your attention somewhere else.

While researching it is important that you remain open to oportunities that are possibly outside your comfort zone. These may well return better yields and although at the start it may be difficult to acclimatise yourself with your purchase, the dividends may be more handsome later on.

At the time I was at my friend's flat in Tooting, I had no compulsion to expand my territory into London. It was, after all, a lot further away than Leeds. It required a new game plan, but other people have done bolder things and so why couldn't I at least have a look at it? So I did. I also changed my game plan halfway through my five-year plan because the market had moved on more quickly than I had expected. It enabled me to seek out other areas that I did not consider. Again that is fine.

Be as flexible as possible when embarking on a new venture. I am not just talking about property, but any business. Markets change so rapidly today that a ten-year plan is almost a complete waste of time if you have to stick to it rigidly in order the see some financial benefit. Our world is not a ten-year plan world anymore. Flexibility means that if change within your business is required, you will not need to completely alter your focus on what it is that you wanted to achieve in the first place. You will merely need to divert your sights to another area, but at least in the same field.

There is no need for you to be afraid of the future if you have been sufficiently careful when getting started. I gave an example of using a rental figure of £400 per month when working out my figures for my Leeds' house. I could of course have used double that to get more money and purchase more, but I dare say that is not the sort of person that I am. I was content to see my single Leeds' seed germinate into something I could be happy with; I did not need to plant an entire garden. It was my first foray into another field and so I was cautious. My next move might well have been in the north again but it turns out that I went south.

The future for property landlords and speculators in this country seems to have hit something of a wall. People are indeed looking abroad for some gains. This will inevitably mean that a market might artificially rise because of the number of people pursuing it. Unfortunately that will mean that there is nothing propping it up and thus it may come crashing down, I am of course referring to areas such as Bulgaria, Romania, the Baltic states, and others that are currently being heralded as emerging markets. For your own sake do not jump on the bandwagon just because you feel that you may get left behind if you don't. That is not a sensible approach nor will it ensure longevity in a business that can indeed deliver, providing you don't rush in.

This book is a rough and basic reflection on a period of my life that takes into account much of what I managed to accomplish in the Nineties and the early part of this century. There was a period when I involved myself with commercial property in the north of England. I bought retail space and offices, the majority of which were on long leases with the local council. One of the reasons that I decided to buy this parade of commercial space was that all the covenants were quite bulletproof. I have not discussed this deal as it really veered away from the bread and butter that was my living, at least until I decided to go on *The Apprentice*. After that things changed, and are continuing to change.

If you have learned anything at all from what I have had to say then please also remember that it may have suited me at the time, but may not you. You and I are different. It is our personalities that will dictate how we go forward in business and in life. Do not fret if you have got off to a slower start than some of your contemporaries. Be content in the knowledge that what you have, or plan to embark on, you are doing at a pace and a level that suits you. A single person in their twenties embarking on a career in property will have far less to lose than a person with a family to consider.

I hope you go on to have as much success in this game as you desire. All I ask is that you have the common courtesy to cut me in to any profit. God bless.

Index